THE QURAN AND THE CONTEMPORARY CHALLENGES

THE QURAN AND THE CONTEMPORARY CHALLENGES

"Surely this Quran guides to that which is most upright. It promises the believers who do good work a rich reward". (Quran 17 : 9)

By
Dr. S.M. Ismail
Edited by
Syed Fazle Rab

COMMONWEALTH PUBLISHERS
NEW DELHI INDIA

The Quran and the Contemporary Challenges

ISBN 81-7169-192-7

Published by:
AJAY VERMA
for **COMMONWEALTH PUBLISHERS**
4378/4-B, MURARI LAL STREET
ANSARI ROAD, DARYAGANJ
NEW DELHI - 110002 (INDIA)
✆ 3272541

Lasertypeset by:
ALFA COMPUTER CENTRE
DA-18, VIKAS MARG,
SHAKARPUR, DELHI - 110092
✆ 2209367

Printed in India at:
EFFICIENT OFFSET PRINTERS
215, SHAHZADA BAGH, PHASE-II
DELHI - 110035

Dedicated
with
Reverence to the pious memory

of

His Holiness, Late Maulana Syed
Mohammed Ali (May blessings
of Allah be on him); the spiritual
Guide of my Late, revered Mother

And

To the pious Memory of my
Late Lamented, Reverent
Mother (May Allah Grant
her place in the abode of
His blessings)
whose
Strict training made me
imbibe the true spirit of
ISLAM.

EDITOR'S NOTE

This manuscript is the outcome of author's long cherished desire to write a book on the teachings of the Holy Quran. The author had worked on it day and night in spite of his prolonged illness as he wanted to get it published as early as possible. Unfortunately, this MSS could not be published in his lifetime because he died on 19th of November, 1991. Since the author was happened to be my father, I consider it my responsibility to take up this pious task. Accordingly, I have arranged it in a way the author wanted it but I owe my full responsibility if there is any mistake left while editing this manuscript. I am really very thankful to Mr. B.R. Varma, the proprietor of the Commonwealth Publishers, New Delhi for bringing out this book in a presentable format in the shortest possible time.

ACKNOWLEDGEMENTS

The author feels highly indebted to the Director General and to Dr. J. Maum, Director Special Programme on AIDS and Mr. E.P. Hoare, Special Programme on AIDS World Health Organisation, Geneva for their prompt response to the author's queries and very kindly sending to the author a number of documents regarding the origin, growth and spread of AIDS and the various actions taken for the check of this dreaded disease throughout the world and their utter disappointment to find out the suitable drug or vaccine to fight this hydra-headed monster.

The author is thankful to Dr. M.K.A. Siddiqui an author of a number of books including the Quran: A Message for all Mankind for kindly going through the manuscript and for his valuable suggestions.

The author feels indebted with love and affection to his eldest son Dr. Syed Fazle Rab, M.A., Ph.D., Librarian, A.N. Sinha Institute of Social Studies and to his eldest daughter-in-law Dr. Semeem Fazal, M.A., Ph.D., B.Ed., B.Lib.Sc., Assistant Librarian of Sinha Library, Patna.

The author has to thank Md. Tajammul Khan for his kind cooperation and creative help for the arrangements of necessary books for writing this volume.

The author also feels very elevated to give his thanks with love and affection to his grand daughter Miss Nishat Zeba a B.A. student and his grand son Syed Toha Owais, his grand daughter Rahatsaba School Student and Syed Shakeel, B.Com. taking down the dictations and taking notes for references for this volume.

The author feels very much indebted to Mr. Jawed Naim who has very affectionately taken pains and care to type this manuscript.

S.M. ISMAIL

PREFACE

1. The basic purpose of writing this volume is mainly to present to our non-Muslim countrymen as well as those living outside this country, the true image of Islam — its fundamentals, its way of worship, its faith in oneness of God, the teachings of the Holy Quran and the sayings of the Holy Prophet (be peace and blessings of Allah on him), to enable them to have the true knowledge of Islam. They may also serve the purpose of reminding the Muslims of the uniqueness of their creed.
2. Unfortunately the image of Islam has been distorted, the truth of Islam has been made opaque, knowledge about Islam has been mischievously confused, confounded and misinterpreted by some biased Christian Missionaries of the west and a section of the British historians, the British administrators and the pro-British writers of fictions and novels in India employed by the British colonialists for this successful pursuit of the British Policy of 'Divide and Rule' and thus to instil and nourish hatred, animosity and ill-will against Muslims by the Hindus in particular.
3. The Christian world is fully aware of the facts that Islam is a true religion of the world and the present age of Science, Medicines, technology, social sciences and Arts owe much to the efforts and contribution of the Muslims. The Muslims were the custodian of the Greeco-Roman learning in every field of Science and Arts and handed over the wealth of learning and scientific thought to Europe which contributed a

good deal to Renaissance in their society. Until then the entire Europe was engulfed in the darkness, illiteracy and ignorance. In this connection it is of paramount importance to quote the observation of Sir Edward Denison Ross in his introduction of the Koran translated by George Sale:

> "I do not wish to imply that Sale did know Arabic, but I do maintain that the work as it stands gives a misleading estimate of his original researchers". (See page VII Introduction of the Koran translated by George Sale)

4. The above observation of Sir Edward Denison Ross will indeed enable the readers to fathom the depth of the evil design and mischievous intention of some Christian Missionaries, Orientalists and Scholars, to distort and misrepresent the facts in order to malign Islam, the Holy Quran and to slander the Holy Prophet. Thus animosity and the ill-will of a section of Christendom against Muslims is still continuing since the 7th century A.D. when the Christians and their crusades suffered innumerable defeats at the hands of the Muslims both politically and militarily with the result that the Muslims were successful as rulers in Spain, France and other places which they conquered. It must be acknowledged that wherever Muslims carried their culture they have been respectful of other systems and have contributed a good deal to the development of the area. They have in fact ushered in an era of glory and splendour. Instead of acknowledging this with gratitude the Christians and westerners continue to harbour a feeling of contempt and have not ceased to strike at the very toproof of Islamic civilization whenever they find an opportunity resorting to concoction and falsehood. Thus very recently they encouraged Rushdie's 'Satanic Verses'

N.B. George Sale (1667-1736) is a very important personality who has translated the Koran into English and is very famous in the Christian world as orientalist.

in order to tarnish the image of Islam and injure the sentiments and feelings of the entire Muslim world and they have themselves blatantly appeared associated with the 'Satanic Verses Episode' to gratify their deep-seated grudge against the Muslims. In this state of affairs the readers must realise how the image of the Muslims have been sought to be blackened by such inhuman irresponsible, injudicious and irrational acts of the so called civilised world, in the west.

There are innumerable instances of the evil designs and the malicious intentions of the west to slander the Holy Prophet Mohammad (be peace and blessings of Allah on him) and they called him, Mohammad, (the imposter and his umma as gullible people to build up a kingdom on earth by the use of power and violence).

The 14th century Italian poet Dante Allghieri consigned him to hell, while Luther described the Pope and the Muslims as the true arch enemies of Christ and his holy chruch. There is a worldwide conspiracy by Jews, Christians, Crusaders, Marxists and western imperialists to undermine the Islamic faith by every possible means from birth control to cultural invasion and intelligence operations. In the west, Muslims are described as lazy, treacherous or violent and fanaticals in cartoons, cheap novels, newspapers and speeches by racist politicians. It must be added here that such malicious and venomous propaganda against Islam is entirely due to the constant defeats and frustrations of the Christians at the hands of the Muslims both in war, conquest and in the fields of learning, culture, Arts, and Science. It is also because Islam alone is against imperialism and lays down the foundation of an egalitarian social order based on love and fraternity. However, in spite of such false propaganda, there are many western scholars who wrote very extensively about the prophet and his teachings which will continue to inspire us. The very purpose of this volume is to present some of the highlights of the life and teachings of the prophet Mohammad (PBUH) based on Quran.

Editor

CONTENTS

1

SHAPING THE MAN

1.1 The training of man through modern curricula

There is no denying the fact that philosophers, eminent thinkers and educationists have been most anxious and sincere in devising the ways and methods for training and educating Man according to the needs of the time. Eminently noted among them are Socrates, Plato, Aristotle (384-322 B.C.), Montesquieu (1689-1753), Ruskin (1810-1900), Russel (1792-1878), Rousseau (1712-78), Herbert Spenser (1820-1903) etc. They all wanted to see man fully equipped with good education and training, so the educational philosophy, educational theories, vocational methodology for the physical, moral and intellectual development of man were introduced to enable him to attain the highest intellectual capability in various spheres of learning including arts and science. This was with the objective of making him a philosopher, a thinker, a statesman, a political leader, a jurist, a law maker, an administrator and a social worker and in the field of science to enable him to become a skilled engineer to build big bridges and dams on the rivers and the seas, to build sky-high buildings, to build big vessels for transport on the water, to train him to dive into water like marine animals, to fly into the air like birds, walk on the surface of the moon, to send and receive messages from one hemisphere to another with ease, to make progress in the world of matters and contribute his mite to the development of science and technology to the extent of inventing deadly weapons like bombs, rockets, missiles and atomic weapons to be kept stored in his arsenals for use at his own sweet will.

1.2 Temple of Learning

No doubt there are millions of temples of learning around the globe with an unimaginable throng of visitors, scholars, scientists, litterateures, investigators, researchers in different fields of scientific activities for the progress of mankind; but sadly enough there are no signs and syndromes discernible showing the existence of God, the Supreme Maker of the universe. His Omnipresence, His Omniscience and His Omnipotence and thus the knowledge and learning so acquired in those temples of learning are motivated to the development of the modern civilization which is entirely materialistic in its nature and its outlook, in its constitution, lacking ingredients. Such materialistic[1] civilization has turned man into a cog in the vast machinery of the world and has also provided favourable environment to the growth of degenerative disorders including fatal disease like Cancers and AIDS as well. This materialistic development of human civilization is not subordinated to spiritual and moral principles and appears to be completely devoid of humanism. This has confronted us with catastrophic situation.

1.3 Impact of Karl Marx

Karl Marx (1818-83) with his Das Capital appeared on the scene and witnessd with horror the sufferings and exploitation of the poor by the rich, by the king, by the Feudal Lords and by the Clergy. The condition of the peasantry and industrial workers was really aweful. This class of population toiled hard in the fields and factories to produce only to fill the exchequer of the king, and to

1. Gilford, Hasting : Tumors and Cancers. London: H.K. Lewis & Co., 1925, p. 388.

provide for the means of luxuries for the Feudal Lords and the clergy as well as the capitalist class. Such pitiable and wretched condition prevailed in the pre-Revolution period as the proletariat was destined to work and toil hard and lead a miserable life of want and poverty while the bourgeois led a life of luxuries and comforts, Karl Marx wanted to do away with this system of inequality in the distribution of wealth. He wanted to put an end to oppression, exploitation and tyranny perpetuated by the rich on the common men, through class-war, class-conflict and blood-shed. He wanted to establish a socialistic pattern of society where all are equal with equal opportunities for the development of their personality. Karl Marx lacked in the faith in the unseen Divinity that regulates, controls, and instils discipline and balance in the work of man, with the result that the class-conflict, class-war, violence and blood-shed and a life for bread and butter only prevailed. A society with gross materialism came into existence with a wide gulf between the bourgeois and the proletariat throughout the world. This in course of time gave rise to the new system of State Capitalist System regimentation in the name of Communism and thus the entire world came to be divided into divergent Blocks, American and Russian and a permanent care for tug of war between the two, and a constant sore for the smaller countries to watch the situation with aweful suspense and apprehension expecting danger any time. 'Might is Right' is the order of the day, with no faith in God, the Creator and Sustainer, the Regulator of universe. This condition of the world can better be linked to a ship without a rudder tossing in the stormy sea finding no destination, ultimately precipitating its own wreck. To sum up, there are rift, disunity, loss of mutual trust, suspense and suspicion-phobia, ill-will, terror, no safety of life, no security of honour and a complete tension in every region of the world and thus the peace, tranquillity and mutual trust and good-will have become the things of the past. The oppressively unbridled capitalism of the west was sought by Marx to be undone by equally oppressive methods totally ignoring better methods for the same objectives which take into account man's accountability to the Supreme Being. The socio-economic programme as laid down by Islam is in sharp contrast to both western capitalism and Marxism.

1.4 Impact of Freud, the Psychoanalysis

It admits of no doubt that the impact of Freud's Psychoanalysis, his theory of Libido and his concept of Oedipus Complex have gone a long way beyond the presincts of morality and decency and to give an erroneous notion to the modern generation about Sex and Sexuality. His psychoanalysis and his theory of Libido have brought in a great turmoil and commotion in the minds of youngsters, in their thinking about sex and induced in them a tendency for the abuse of the sexual instincts to an unimaginable extent. Thus the unbridled outlet of their sexual passion with imbalance and perversion, including biological transgression as homosexuality, promiscuity, hetero-sexuality, incest, prostitution, whoredom have become the order of the day with a terrible consequence of drug addiction and intoxication including alcoholism and these immoral acts have given rise to venereal diseases of syphilis and gonorrhoea and other sexuality transmitted diseases like Cancers and AIDS and (H.I.V.) Acquired Immuno Deficiency Syndrome which are taking a heavy toll of millions of human lives inflicting agony and pain to the horror and dismay of the medical scientists who are at their best efforts to discover some suitable medicines to give relief to such miserable victims. Thus sexuality without religiosity provides licence to enjoy whereas sexuality with religiosity gives liberty to enjoy for achieving the sacred purpose of procreation and moral satisfaction.

1.5 The Work of the Social Scientists

A society with a misguided political, economical, social and sexual thinking with an erroneously misunderstood concept of life, with the impact and the influence of so many isms — capitalism, communalism, socialism, imperialism, materialism, skepticism, sexualism, alcoholism, above all terrorism with the total lack of idealism, humanism, and spiritualism — is destined to be anarchic, chaotic, degenerative with no fear for the law of the State, with no scruple for the norms of the society, with no respect for the human blood — a society with schizophrenia, mental illness, amentia, dementia, insanity, perversion, massochism, sadism, sexual imbalance, promiscuity, drug addiction, intoxication with a milieu of pornography, prostitution, whoredom, homosexuality, and heterosexuality with no consideration of kindred in the gratification of sexual urge (incest) with illegal birth of children, swindling, cheating, defrauding one another, bloodshed and violence of unimaginable extent etc. At this gloomy and baffling situation of the modern society, the work of the Social Scientists is very colossal, heavy and pains-taking to do away with the ills of the existing society. It admits of no doubt that the social thinkers of the ancient and medieval age and the social scientists of the Eighteenth, Nineteenth and Twentieth Centuries have left no stone unturned for the reform of the society. The holding of the seminars, symposia and group discussions at regional, national, and international levels to find out the real cause of the degenerating conditions of the society, but to their utter despair and dismay nothing concrete could be achieved in this regard. It would not be out of place to quote the words of Dr. D.G. Gran, his book "The Key to the Science of Man."[2] Man is a product of nature. He is an organism that maintains physiologically, a state normal for its species and itself, uniformally precise to tiniest details. Thus man is expected to obey rigorously the Divine Law. He is the vicegerent of God. He must recognise His Supremacy, His Omniscience, His Omnipotence and His Omnipresence. He must regulate

2. Gran, D.G. "The Key to the Science of Man", Philosophical Library, New York, 1975, p. 26.

his actions in accordance with the Divine bordain, with the fear of the punishment of God Herein and Hereafter. This is the only key to regulate the normalcy and equilibrium of the human life. Man has been constantly changing the natural environment. Industrialisation, urbanisation, change in socio-political institutions etc. are among the factors responsible for maladjustments in human society and all these have to be reckoned with to solve the problems. The task will be difficult unless a deep seated feeling of destiny and ultimate accountability is ingrained in every one concerned.

1.6 Influence of Science and Scientific Thought

A. Science defined : "Science may be defined as describing, creating, and understanding facts of human experience" (Lindsay). It would be well-nigh impossible to achieve this object unless we evolve a 'system' or 'method' to study the countless phenomena of the universe such as the grandeur of the starlit sky, the blaze of the burning sun, the beauty and fragrance of flowers, the moon, the stars, the planets, the solar system, the high up mountains, the deep seas, the change of the day into night and vice versa, the change in weather, the movement of the earth, the sun, the moon and the other planets in the sky with the most disciplined and co-ordinated way and other countless mysteries in nature. Perhaps it would be better to say that science is an activity pursued by means of scientific methods.

B. Scientific method, or the Scientific methodology : There are four steps in the scientific methodology:

(i) The Experimental Data
(ii) Law
(iii) Hypothesis
(iv) Theory

C. The main branches of science are : (1) Physics, the investigation of Energy and its transformation (2) Chemistry, the investigation of Matter and its transformation (3) Biology, the investigation of Living Things.

D. The Work of Science : Matter and spirit should be reconciled — The nexus of these three branches of science, physics, chemistry and biology, is interdependent and inseparable and this has enabled man to conquer the material world and unravel the mysteries of nature by dint of his continued and constant labour with strong will and firm determination and dogged pursuit of his undertakings in varied variety of researches and investigations. His flight in the air like bird, his dive deep in the bottom of the seas like marine animal, his dig into the lowest strata of the earth, his building of big dams and bridges of the seas and rivers, his constructing sky high building, his climbing on the highest peak of the mountains, his walking on the surface of the moon, his controlling of the ferocious and wild animals so dexterously, are no doubt worthy of admiration; but it must be borne in mind that the mere conquest of the material world without the achievement of the spiritual forces is absolutely soulless, purposeless and goalless because the real purpose of science and scientific thought is to remove the hindrance in the way of true development of man's personality by harnessing the forces latent in his nature in such a way as to broaden his life and make it rich in all aspects of matter and spirit.

E. The task and responsibility of the modern scientist : The work of the modern scientists is highly important, responsible, multi-directional and potentially useful and rational for the benefits of mankind. The gross materialism in the world of science and the scientific knowledge without the world of spiritualism is mainly responsible for the ills and maladies of the present day society. Materialism and spiritualism should be interdependent and inseparable. They cannot be isolated and separated. If so, there will be catastrophe, anarchy, lawlessness, degenerative disorders, imbalance in thinking and irrationality in doing, with the result that the entire would will be engulfed in darkness despite the so called material affluence and prosperity.

F. Duty of scientist : Scientists have made researches, investigations and tried to unravel the mysteries in the various phenomena of nature and natural objects in the process of observations, examination and making analysis, he must have come across the finest, most delicate, and most intricate details of the mechanism of the Universe beyond comprehension of mankind that have led to believe spontaneously, the existence of its Maker, the Supreme Power, who has created this Universe as He Himself announces in His Holy Book, the Quran, in the following verses:

> "Most surely Allah has power over everything, O mankind, submit to your Lord, Who created you and those who were before you; in this way only you may expect to save yourselves. It is He Who has made the earth a bed for you and the sky a canopy, and it is He Who sends down rain from above for the growth of every kind of food products for your sustenance. So, when you know this you should not set up equals to rank Allah" (Al-Baqarah 1 : 21-22) "And if you be in doubt whether the Book (Quran) We have sent down to our servant is from Us not, then produce, at least one Surah like this you may call your associates to assist you and avail yourselves of the help, of anyone other than Allah. If you are of genuine (in your doubt, do this). But if you do not do this, and you can never do this, then fear the fire which has been prepared for the disbelievers and which shall have men and stones for fuel". (Al-Baqarah 1 : 23-24).

At other place in the Quran God declares:

> "And He has made subservient to you the sun and the moon pursuing their curses and He has made subservient to you the night and the day".

The truth of the sayings of the Quran is recognized and declared by Dr. Maurice Bucaille, a French Surgeon in these words:

> "Those who seek among modern data for proof of the variety of the Holy Scripture will find magnificent illustration of the verses of the Quran dealing with the Pharoah's body by visiting the Royal Mummes Rooms of the Egyptian Museum,

Cairo.[3] Thus the findings of the modern Research are enough to disprove the Darwinian Theory of the Evolution in to-to".

Similarly John Wilson in his book "Philosophy and Religion (London 1861) has expressed his ideas about the existence of God in the following lines :

"This does not destroy my behalf: It is still God working through these things who is responsible for the tides."[4]

These scientists, as a matter of fact, with their scientific imagination, with their scientific knowledge, scientific experience, scientific intuition and with scientific eyes, can be very well in a position to give a clarion call to the present day society of the modern world with these words :

Praise is only for Allah, the Lord of the Universe, the All-compassionate, the All Merciful, the Master of the Day of Judgement. The alone we worship and to Thee alone we pray for help. Show us the straight way the way of those whom Thou hast blessed; who have not incurred Thy Wrath, not gone astray. (Al-Fatihah 1 : 1-7)

1.7 **Praise is only for Allah**

The spirit enshrined in the above prayer will go a long way to remove the evils and vices of the modern society and establish peace, harmony, trust and good will throughout the international community for which the international community, the social scientists, the social organisations including the United Nations Organisation are anxious for the achievement of this goal. This clarion call of the scientists of this effect will undoubtedly clear all the misgivings and doubts about the existence of God, His Omnipotence, His Omniscience and His Omnipresence and thus there will be a thorough change in the thinking

3. P. 242 The Bible, The Quran and Science, 1976 (Please also see footnote 4 under para 4.15 of the book).
4. Quoted in Muzhab and Science (Urdu) by Maulana Wahiduddin Khan, Maktaba Al-Resala, Nazmat Building, Qasim Jan Street, Delhi, 1980, p. 38.

and doing of the present day society with the result that lawlessness, anarchy, terrorism and barbarity will be effaced from the face of the earth and the earth will be worth living with peace and tranquillity all round with emphasis on the harmonious combination of Matter and Spirit.

2

THE PROPHET

It is, indeed, a fact that the biographical literature about the Holy Prophet is quite substantial. A great deal of these have been written by a number of authors, scholars and historians, including Christian Missionaries in a number of languages such as French, Greek, German, Spanish, English and Arabic etc. "Many of them are competent, some absolutely excellent."[1] It is indeed a striking fact that no such great and vast biographies, and lives of other Prophets have been attempted at. These biographies of the Holy Prophet Mohammad (be peace and blessings of Allah on him) have been mostly written by non-Muslim writers of the west with pre-conceived and pre-planned ideas of criticising, slandering and speaking ill of this great personality and at the same time most of them had to admire his nobleness, truthfulness, simplicity, love and affection for both friends and foes, universal brotherhood, peace, non-violence, fellow-feelings, respect for women and love for children. "The smallest details of his behaviour served as a model for all to follow. Of course, standards of ideas could be defended by attributing their origin to his words or actions. He had laid down the rules for divorce and for government just as he had shown how one should behave one's self at table, below one's nose or

1. Rodinson, Maxime 'Mohammed' translated by Anne Carger, published in Great Britain, 1971, p. ix.

make love". "As a man, he had been perfect and beyond criticism."[2] Space does not permit to mention all about the life of the Holy Prophet (be peace and blessings of Allah on him).

2.1 Mecca, an urban centre in the Arabian Peninsula, is the birth place of the Prophet

The Prophet Mohammad was born in the year 571 A.D. in the family of a tribe known as the 'Quraish'. It was a well to do and influential family in the city of Mecca. His father's name was Abdullah who died a few months before he was born and his mother died when he was only six years old.

2.2 His care and nourishment

It fell first to his grand father to take care of him and then to his uncle Abu Talib.

2.3 He was called Ameen (The Trustworthy), because from his early youth he impressed his countrymen as a person of high integrity, and gentle disposition, painfully sensitive to human sufferings, he was much loved in his small circle.[3]

2.4 His early life

His early life was not free from the burden of labour, for Abu Talib was not rich, like his ancestors, and the younger members of the family had to take their turn in tending the flocks and herds.

2.5 His meditation

From early youth Mohammad (B.P.U.H.) was given to meditation. He spent a month every year in meditation and spiritual communion in a cave in Mount Hira, not far off from Mecca. One night as he lay in the cave wrapped in his mantle, God spoke to his soul through a messenger—

2. Ibid. p. 302.
3. Ali, Syed Ameen, Short History of the Saracens. London, Macmillan, 1927, p. 28.

Jibraeel to arise and preach to his people. Henceforth, his life is devoted to the task of raising them from degradation, of making them given up their evil ways and of teaching them their duty to their fellow-beings.

2.6 Muhammad's Divine Call

Muhammad's Divine Call began in 610 A.D. when he, while engaged in meditation in the above mentioned cave, received the first of a long series of revelations, which continued to be revealed in portions and on occasions until his death in 632 A.D. In these revelations Muhammad was warned that God had chosen him as His apostle and that he was charged with the task of communicating His message to mankind.

2.7 The social condition prevailing in Arabia at that time

The social condition in Arabia then was most evil and deplorable. The whole of Arabia was engulfed in darkness, in illiteracy, gambling, wine-drinking, infanticide,[4] enmity and animosity, ill-feelings against own fellow brothers. Though most of the Arabians were idol-worshippers, some followed Christianity and Judaism. But the overall condition of the whole of Arabia was miserable and most inhuman, persons felt delight and pride in slandering other people, in killing their daughters, in stealing things belonging to other people and committing wicked and evil acts, adultery, fornication and intoxication were rampant. The people led a very miserable, deprived and degraded life always quarrelling and fighting each other with no brotherly feeling for fellow-brothers. Even those who claimed to follow Christianity and Judaism distorted the teachings of their religion.

2.8 His marriage with Khadija

When Muhammad (B.P.U.H.) was twenty five years old, he married Khadija, a wealthy and noble widow who

4. Infanticide was frequent among the pre-Islamic Arabs (Amir Ali).

had engaged him to handle her carven trade, and who had developed great admiration and respect for his noble character.

2.9 A happy marriage

Khadija was a noble broad minded lady with good understanding and consequently the marriage proved to be a happy one. Though during the first fifteen years of their marriage, 595-610 A.D., he would retire for days to the cave 'Hira' for meditation and spiritual devotion, she never complained, and always welcomed him back home when in 610 A.D. he received his Divine Call. She was the first to recognise him as the Apostle of Allah and to convert to Islam, remaining until her death in 620 A.D.

2.10 His children

They had several children, all the sons died in infancy, but the daughters lived to see the great mission of their father's life. The youngest Fatima, surnamed as zahra, "the beautiful" was married to Hazrat Ali, the son of Abu Talib.

2.11 His Marriage after the death of Khadija

After the death of Khadija, Muhammad (be peace and blessings of Allah on him), in accordance with Arab customs and the old patriarchal ways, married several wives, partly with the object of uniting hostile tribes, and partly to provide means of subsistence to helpless women.[5]

2.12 His career as Prophet

Muhammad's career as Prophet lasted for about 23 years, about half of which he spent in Mecca and the other in Madinah, which lies about 280 miles north of Mecca.

5. This is a befitting answer to the malicious propaganda of the Christians that he himself married nearly fourteen wives but asked his followers to marry only four wives.

2.13 His migration or Hijrat[6] to Medina (622 A.D.)

During the first period, his efforts to win the Meccans to Islam met with vehement opposition. The Meccans became so violent, furious and even attacked his life. He had, therefore, to emigrate along with the few followers, who had been able to convert. to Medina in 622 A.D. from which dates the Mohammadan Calendar.

2.14 Warm welcome at Madinah

The Holy Prophet was given a hearty and warm welcome at Madinah and moved from one success to another in the spread of Islam, the message of peace, non-violence and universal brotherhood far and wide.

2.15 His death in 632 A.D.

By the time he died in 632 A.D. he had united all Arabia under the banner of Islam and completed his message to mankind.

2.16 The sources of Islam

The two main sources of Islam are the Quran and the Sunnah or the way of the Prophet which include his sayings, actions and tacit approval of things said and done in his presence. The acceptance and understanding of the Prophet's legacy is essential in Islam, because first its acceptance is enjoined by Allah in the Quran and second it supplements and explains the Quranic message.

2.17 Islam, a dynamic force

Islam spread with dynamic force among the human habitations of both the Northern and Southern hemispheres of the globe. The dynamic force is because of its true message of peace, non-violence, universal brotherhood, spirit of self-sacrifice, services to mankind, to help the

6. The "Hijira" or the year of the Hijrat was instituted seventeen years later by second Caliph.
7. Sale, George, Koran, London: Fredrick Warne & Co., 1934, p. vii.

needy and the poor to have respect for human rights, respect for other religions, love, and compassion for weak, sick, infirm old people, women and children without any discretion of caste and creed, nationality and colour, and absolute submission to the invisible God, the Almighty, in His Oneness, in His Omniscience, in His Omnipotence, in His Omnipresence, an absolute faith in the enjoinments of the Holy Quran and to regulate all thoughts and actions according to teachings of the Holy Quran as well as according to the teachings of the Holy Prophet. Under the impact of Islam, the Muslims were virile, dynamic, bold, fearless, true, honest, trustworthy and were successful in every walk of life whether in war or in peace. They took part in the development of art and learning, science and culture, statesmanship and administration and thus Islam's contribution to material and spiritual progress is vast. Some of the honest and sensible writers of the west could not help admiring the way and teachings of Islam. One of them is Sir Edward Denison Ross, who has expressed his sentiments about Islam in his introduction of the Koran, translated by George Sale in the following words:

> "Islam although seriously affecting the Christian world brought a spiritual religion to one half of Asia."

There is no denying the fact that Islam in reality has brought about a dynamic change in the emotional, intellectual, moral and spiritual well-being of man not only in Asia but throughout the human world.

3

THE QURAN

3.1 The revelation of the Quran

The Quran was revealed to Mohammad (be peace and blessings of Allah on him) of Arabia nearly fourteen hundred years ago, in the beginning of the Seventh Century A.D.

3.2 The subject it deals[1]

The subject it deals with is MAN; it discusses those aspects of man's life that lead either to his real success or failure.

3.3 The central theme

The central theme that runs throughout the Quran is the exposition of the Reality and the invitation of the Right way based on it. It declares that the Reality is the same that was revealed by Allah Himself to Adam at the time of his appointment as the vicegerent, and to all the Messengers after him, and the Right way is the same that was taught by all the Messengers of Allah. It also points out that all theories, contradictory to this Reality, invented by people about God, the Universe, Man and his relations with God and the rest of His creation, are all wrong and that all the ways of life based on them are erroneous and lead to ruinous consequences.

1. Maudoodi, Syed Abul Ala, The meaning of the Quran, Vol. I, Delhi, Markazi Maktaba Islami, 1982, p. 10.

3.4 The aims and objects of the revelation

The aim and object of the revelations is to invite Man to that Right path and to present clearly those teachings which he has lost because of his negligence or has perverted them by his wickedness.

3.5 Background of revelations

One cannot understand fully many of the topics discussed in the Quran unless one is acquainted with the background of the revelation. One should know the social, historical, or other antecedents or conditions which help to explain any particular topic. For, the Quran was not revealed as a complete book at once and at the same time; nor did Allah hand over a written copy of it to Muhammad (be peace of Allah on him) at the very beginning of his mission and command him to publish it and invite people to adopt a particular way of life. The Quran adopts its own style to suit the guidance of the Islamic Movement that was started by Allah's Messenger under His direct command. Accordingly, Allah revealed the Quran piece-meal to meet the requirements of the Movement in its different stages at different times.

3.6 Places of revelation of the Quran

The Quran was revealed at Makkah and at Al-Madinah.

3.7 The Makki Surahs

When the Holy Prophet was commanded to start his mission at Mecca, Allah sent down such instructions as the Messenger needed for his training for the great work that was entrusted to him. The Quran also imparted the basic knowledge of Reality and gave brief answer to the common misunderstandings that misled the people to adopt wrong ways of life and invited them to accept the basic principles of morality and adopt righteous attitude that alone leads to the success and welfare of humanity.

3.8 **The early messages at Makkah**

The early messages consisted of short and concise sentences and were couched in a very fluent and effective language to suit the taste of the people to whom they were first addressed. Their excellent literary style was so appealing that it touched their very hearts. They were so charming that they attracted the attention of the hearers, who began to repeat them because of their beauty and elegance. Though universal truth was enunciated in these messages they are given a local colour and were supported by arguments, examples and illustrations from the environment with which its first addresses were quite familiar. In order to make the address impressive these early addresses were confined to their own history, their traditions, their movements, their beliefs, their morality, and their evil ways.

3.9 **Period of revelation of Makkah**

The early Surahs were revealed at Makkah and they cover a period of thirteen years.

3.10 **Madani Surahs**

After facing opposition for thirteen years, in Makkah the Islamic Movement found a new centre in Al-Madinah where it became possible to collect all its followers from the various parts of Arabia and to unify and strengthen them. Accordingly, the Holy Prophet and the majority of the Muslims migrated to Al-Madinah. Now that the Muslim community had succeeded in establishing a regular state, an armed encounter ensued with the upholders and exponents of the old order of ignorance. Besides this, the Jews and the Christians came into conflict with it even though they also professed to be the followers of Prophet. It had also to deal with different kind of hypocrite 'Muslims' who had somehow or other entered its fold. But in spite of all these obstacles, the Movement succeeded in subduing the whole of Arabia after a hard struggle of ten years and was in a position to extend its universal message of reform to the outer world. This is the background of the Surahs that were revealed during the ten years at Al-Madinah.

3.11 Number of Siparahs and Surahs

The Quran consists of thirty Siparahs (Parts) and one hundred and fourteen Surahs (Chapters) of unequal length. The longest Surah has 285 verses and the shortest only three.[2]

3.12 The Quran, a Divine Guidance

The Holy Quran is a divine guidance for man. Whether one believes it to be a revealed book or not one will have to consider, as a starting point, the claim that is put forward by itself and its bearer, Muhammad (Allah's peace be upon him) that this is the Divine Guidance.[3]

3.13 Emphasis on the reflection of Laws of Nature

The Quran emphasises reflection on the Laws of Nature with examples drawn from cosmology, physics, biology and medicine as sign for all men.[4] Thus:

> "Can they not look up to the clouds, how they are created; and to the Heaven how it is upraised; and the mountains how they are rooted, and to the earth how it is outspread ?"
>
> (88 : 17)

and again,

> "Verily in the creation of the heavens and of the earth, and in the alternation of the night and of the day, are there signs of men of understanding."
>
> (3 : 189-90)

> "Seven hundred and fifty verses of the Quran — almost (one eighth of the Book) — exhorts believers to study Nature, to

2. Lings, Martin, 'Muhammad', Lahore, Evergreen Press, 1983, p. 48.
3. Maudoodi, Syed Abul Ala, *op. cit.* p. 8.
4. Abdus Salam, Ideals and Realities, Singapore, World Scientific, 1987, p. 180.

reflect, to make the best use of reason in their search for the ultimate and to make the acquiring of knowledge and scientific comprehension, part of the community life."

"The Holy Prophet of Islam (Peace be on him) emphasised that the quest for knowledge and study of science is obligatory upon every Muslim man and woman. This is the first premise on scientific knowledge with which any fundamentalist thinking in Islam must begin. And to this the second premise — eloquently reinforced by Maurice Bucaille in his essay on "The Bible, the Quran and Science." "There is not a single verse in the Quran where natural phenomena are described and which contradicts what we know for certain from our discoveries in sciences."[5]

Add to this third premise: "in Islamic history there has been no incident like that of Galileo. Persecution, excommunication (takfeer) which unfortunately continues even to day over doctrinal difference but not to my knowledge, directly for scientific beliefs."[6]

3.14 The Quran through the unlettered Prophet is itself a miracle and truth

"And thou was not able to recite a Book before this, nor art thou able to transcribe it with the right hand. In that case, indeed would the talker of vanities have doubted. Nay, there are the Signs, self-evident in the hearts of those endowed with knowledge and none but the unjust reject our Signs. Yet they say, "Why are not the Signs sent down to him from his Lord," Say, "the Signs are indeed with God and I am a clear Warner". And is not enough for them that we have sent down to them the Book which is rehearsed to them? Verily it is mercy and a reminder to those who believe". (29 Ankabut-48-51).

5. Bucaille, Maurice, The Bible, the Quran and Science, Tripoli, World Islamic Call Society (n.d.).
6. P 19 Arberry, A.G. Revelation and Reason in Islam (George Allen and Unwin, London) quoted from Abdus Salam, Ideals and Realities (World Scientific, Singapore, 1987, p. 180.

3.15 Opinion of Dr. Maurice Bucaille — a French Scholar and Medical Practitioner in respect of the authenticity of the Holy Quran

"In view of the state of knowledge in Mohammad's day, it is inconceivable that many of the statements in the Quran which are connected with science could have been the work of a man. It is, morever, perfectly legitimate, not only to regard the Quran as the expression of a Revelation, but also to award it a very special place, on account of the guarantee of authenticity it provides and the presence in its scientific statements which, when studied to-day, appear as a challenge to human explanation."[7]

3.16 The Book of Allah

"This is the Book of Allah: there is no doubt about it. It is guidance to God-fearing people, who believe in the unseen, establish salat and expend (in our way) out of what we have bestowed upon them, who believe in the Book we have sent down to you and in the Books sent down before you and firmly believe in the Hereafter, such people are on the right way from their Lord and such are truly successful." (Al-Baqarah 2 : 4, 5)

3.17 Quran the Scripture from Allah

And if you be in doubt whether the Book We have sent down to Our servant is from Us or not, then produce at least, One Surah like this. You may call all your associates to assist you and avail yourselves of the help of any one other than Allah. If you are genuine (in your doubt do this). But if you do not do this, and you can never do this, then fear the Fire which has been prepared for disbelievers and which shall have men and stones for fuel". (Al-Baqarah 2 : 23-24)

7. Bucaille, Maurice, The Bible, The Quran and Science. Translated from the French by Al Stair D. Panncell and the Author Edition Seghers, 6 Place Saint-Sulprice, 75006, France Published by the Great Socialist - People's Libyan Arab Jamahirayah Tripoli, p. 269.

3.18 Protection of the Quran

Surely We have revealed the Reminder and We will be most surely its guardian (Al-Hijir 15 : 9)

3.19 Allah has power over everything

Most surely Allah has power over everything. O Mankind, submit to your Lord who created you and those who were before you, in this way only you may expect to save yourselves. It is He Who has made the earth a bed for you and the sky a canopy; and it is He Who sends down rain from above for the growth of every kind of food products for your sustenance. So, when you know this you should not set up equals to rank with Allah." (Al-Baqarah 2 : 21-22).

3.20 God is Omnipotent

"Dost thou know that God has power over all things? Dost thou know that to God belong the domain or the heavens and the earth and that besides Him thou hast neither a guardian nor a helper". (Quran 2 : 107-108)

3.21 God is Omniscient and Omnipresent

"With Him are the keys of the unseen, that treasures that none knoweth but He. He knoweth whatever there is on the earth and in the seas. Not a leaf doth fall but with His knowledge. There is not a grain in the darkness (or depths) of the earth nor anything fresh or dry or green or withered but is inscribed in a record clear (to those who can read)". (Quran 3 : 59)

3.22 God is Eternal and Absolute

"Say He is God, the One and Only God, the Eternal and the Absolute. He begotteth not, nor is He begotten; there is none up to him". (Quran 95 : 1-4)

3.23 God knows all

"Say, whether Ye hide what is in your heart or reveal it, God knoweth it all. He knoweth what is in the heavens and what is in the earth and God has power over all things." (3 : 29)

3.24 Everything belongs to God

"Say, my prayer and my sacrifice and my life and my death are all for God, the Cherisher and Nourisher of all the worlds". (6 : 163)

3.25 Trust in God

"If God helps you, none can overcome you; if he forsakes you, who is thereafter that, that can help you? In God, then, let believers put their trust". (3 : 160)

3.25A Do not walk on the earth with insolence

"And do not walk on the earth with insolence, for thou canst rend it as under nor reach the mountains in height". (17 : 37)

3.25B Say a right word

"O, ye who believe fear God and (always) say a word directed to the Right." (33 : 70)

3.26 Worthy of honour in the sight of God

"Truly the most worthy of honour in the sight of God is he who feareth Him most." (49 : 13 in part)

3.27 Seek help with patience, perseverance and prayer

"O Believers, seek help with fortitude and Salat for Allah is with those who show fortitude. And do not say of those who are slain in the way of Allah, "They are dead". In fact they are alive but you do not perceive that life. We will surely put you to trial by involving you in fear and hunger and by causing loss of property, life and earnings. And give good tidings to those who remain steadfast in these trials; when a misfortune comes to them, they say "We are A-llah's and we shall certainly return to Him". Their Lord will bestow great blessings and mercy upon them; such are the people who are rightly guided. (Quran 2 : 153-157)

3.28 **Prayer, sacrifice, life and death are all for God**

"Say, my prayer and my sacrifice and my life and my death are all for God the Cherisher and Nourisher of all the worlds". (6 : 163)

3.29 **The Light of the Iman (Belief)**

"With the light of the Iman lit in your heart, the path in front of you lies fully illumined and you can reach your destination without any difficulty. The Iman is the light of all lights. Every light can reach only a certain distance beyond which there is darkness. But the light of the Iman leaves no darkness at all. You can see the entire world in its true perspective and also the Hereafter, calling you to unknown bliss, a just reward for those who are pleased with God and with whom God is pleased". As God Himself says, "This is a day on which the truthful will profit by their truth. They shall have gardens in which rivers flow to abide in them for ever. God is well pleased with them and they with God and this is the mighty achievement". (5 : 119)

3.30 **Do not exceed the limit**

"O you who believe do not forbid (yourselves) the good things which Allah has made lawful for you and do not exceed the limits." (5:87) Balance and moderation is the keynote in the Quran and transcending the limits is always forbidden.

3.31 **Be careful of your duty and do good to others**

"On those who believe and do good there is no blame for what they eat, when they are careful (of their duty) and believe and do good deeds, then they are careful (of their duty) and believe, then they are careful (of their duty) and do good (to others) and Allah loves those who do good (to others)". (5 : 93)

3.32 **Nothing is hidden from Allah**

"Nothing in the Earth or in the heavens is hidden from Allah. It is He Who shapes you in the wombs of your mothers as He wills. There is no deity but He, the Almighty, the Allwise. It is He Who has sent down this Book to you. There are two kinds of verses in this Book. Muhkamat (which are precise in meaning) they are the essences of the Book, and the other kind is mutashabihat (which are ambiguous). Those, who are perverse of heart always go after the mutashabihat in pursuit of mischief and try to interpret them arbitrarily, whereas in fact, none save Allah knows their real meaning." In contrast to them, those, who possess sound knowledge, say, "We believe in them because all of them are from our Lord." And the fact is that only people of insight can learn lessons from such things. They pray to Allah "Our Lord, let not our hearts become perverse after thou hast once guided us aright, bestow upon us mercy from Thyself for Thou are the real Benefactor Lord; Thou will surely gather all mankind together on a Day which is inevitable; for Thou never failest to fulfil Thy promise". (Al-e-Imran : 5-9)

3.33 **Allah created the heavens and the earth**

"Allah created the heavens and the earth with truth; most surely there is a sign in this for the believers". (29 : 44)

3.34 **Prayer keeps away from indecency and evil**

"Recite that which has been revealed to you of the Book and keep up prayer; Surely prayer keeps (one) away from indecency and evil, and certainly the remembrance of Allah is the greatest and Allah knows what you do." (29 : 45)

3.35 **Every soul must meet death**

"Every soul must taste death, then to Us you shall be brought back."

"And (as far) those who believe and do good, We will certainly give them abode in the high places in the gardens beneath which rivers flow, abiding therein; how good the reward of the workers."

"Those who are patient, and on their Lord do they rely."

"And how many a living creature that does not carry its sustenance; Allah sustains it and yourselves; and He is the Hearing, the knowing."

"And if you ask them Who created the heavens and the earth and made the sun, and the moon subservient, they will certainly say, Allah, Whence are they then turned away"? (29 : 57-58-59-60-61)

3.36 **Things prohibited**

"Say; come I will rehearse what God hath really prohibited from you. Joint not anything as equal with Him, be good to your parents and kill not your children for fear of poverty; we provide sustenance for you and for them; come not nigh to shameful deeds whether open or secret, and take not life which God hath made except by way of justice; thus doth He command you that ye may learn wisdom. And come not nigh to the orphan's property except to improve it, until he attains the age of full strength; give full measure and weight with justice; no burden do We place on any soul but that which it can bear; whenever ye speak, speak justly, even if a near relative is concerned, and fulfil the covenant of God; thus doth He command you that ye may remember. Verily this is My way, leading straight; follow it and follow not other paths; thus doth he command ye that ye may be righteous." (6: 151-153)

3.37 **Messenger of God**

(A) "God did confer a great favour on the believers when He sent among them a messenger from among themselves rehearsing unto them the signs of God, sanctifying them and instructing them in Scripture and wisdom while before that they had been in manifest error". (3 : 164)

(B) "Those who obey God and His Messenger will be admitted into Gardens, with rivers flowing beneath, to abide therein for ever and this will be the supreme achievement." (4 : 13)

(C) "We sent thee not but as a mercy to all creatures". (21 : 197)

"Ye have indeed in the Messenger of God a beautiful pattern of conduct for anyone whose hope is in God and the Final Day and who engages much in the praise of God". (33 : 21)

"God and His angels send blessing on the Prophet. O ye that believe, send ye blessing on him and salute him with all respect." (33 : 56)

3.38 **Worship God and be kind to parents**

"The Lord hath decreed that ye workship none but Him and that ye be kind to parents. Whether one or both of them attain old age in their life, say not to them a word of contempt nor repel them but address them in terms of honour. And out of Kindness, lower to them the wings (shoulders) of humility and say, 'My Lord', bestow on them Thy Mercy even as they cherished me in childhood". (17-23-24)

"And render to the kindred their due rights, as also to those in want, and to the way-farer. But squander not thy wealth in the manner of a spendthrift." (17 : 26)

3.29 **God created man out of mere clot of congealed blood**

"Proclaim in the name of the Lord and Cherisher who created man out of mere clot of congealed blood. Proclaim And thy Lord is most Bountiful. He who taught the use of the Pen taught man that which he knew not. Nay, but man doth transgress all bounds, in that be looketh upon himself as self-sufficient". (Iqraa 76 : 1-7)

3.40 **All Apostles were but men**

"Before thee also the apostles we sent were but men to whom We granted inspiration. If you realise this not, ask of those who possess the Message. Nor did we give them bodies that ate no food nor were they exempt from death" (21 Anbya 7-8). The apostles were all human and members of their society, chosen by Allah to guide mankind and to show them the right path.

And they say, "What sort of apostle is this who eats food and walks through the streets ? Why an angel has not been sent down to him to give admonition or why a treasure has not been bestowed upon him or why he has not a garden for enjoyment"? The wicked say "Ye follow none other than a man bewitched." See, what kind of comparisons, they make for thee. But they have gone astray and never a way will they be able to find". (25 Furqan 7-9) The apostle of Allah were not superhuman and in many ways they behaved like human beings.

3.41 **Prophet Muhammad Mercy for all Creatures**

"We sent thee not but as a Mercy for all creatures. Say "What has come to me by inspiration is that your God is One God. Will ye therefore bow to His will in Islam ? But if they turn back, say, "I have proclaimed the message to you all alike and in truth but I know not whether that which ye are promised in near or far. It is He who knows that is open in speech and what ye hide in your hearts. I know not but that it may be a trial for you and a grant of worldly livelihood to you for a time". (21 Anbya 107-11)

3.42 **The Resurrection**

"O mankind if ye have a doubt about the Resurrection, consider that We created you out of dust, then out of sperm, then out of a leech like clot then out of a morsel of flesh, partly formed and partly unformed in order that We may nanifest Our Power to you and We cause whom We will to rest in the wombs for an appointed term, then do We bring you out as babes, then foster you that you may reach your age of full strength and some of you are called to die and some are sent back to the feeblest old age, so that they know nothing after having known much; and further thou seest the earth barren and lifeless, but when

We pour down rain on it, it is stirred to life; it swells and pours forth every kind of beautiful growth in pairs. This is so because God is the Reality, it is He Who gives life to the dead, and it is He Who has power over all things. And verily the Hour will come; there can be no doubt about it or about the fact that God will raise up all who are in the graves. Yet there is among men such a one as disputes about God without knowledge, without guidance and without a Book of Enlightenment — Disdainfully bending his side, in order to lead them astray from the Path of God. For him there is disgrace in this life and on the Day of Judgement We shall make him taste the Penalty of burning Fire. It will be said, "This is because of the deeds which the hands sent forth, for verily God is not unjust to His servants". (22 Hajj 5-10)

3.43 **If there were other Gods beside God**

"If there were in the heavens and the earth other Gods besides God, there would have been confusion in both. But glory to God, the Lord of the throne : High is He, above what they attribute to Him". (21 Anbya 22)

"O men. Here is a parable set forth. Listen to it. These on whom besides God ye call, cannot create even a fly, if they all met together for the purpose and if the fly should snatch away anything from them, they would have no power to release it from the fly. Feeble are those who petition and those whom they petition. No just estimate have they made of God, for God is He who is strong and able to carry out His will." (22 Hajj 75-76)

"O, ye who believe, bow down, prostrate yourselves, and adore your Lord and do good that ye may prosper. And strive in His cause as you ought to strive. He has chosen you and has imposed no difficulties on you in religion; it is the cult of your father Abraham. It is He who has named you Muslims both before and in this Revelation; that the Apostle may be a witness for you and ye may be witness for mankind. So establish regular prayer, give regular charity and hold fast to God. He is your Protector — the Best to protect and the Best to help". (22 Hajj 77-78)

3.44 **To God Sincere Devotion is due**

"Is it not to God that sincere devotion is due? But those who take for protectors other than God say "We only serve them in order that they may bring us nearer to God". Truly God will judge between them in that wherein they differ. But God guides not such as are false and ungrateful". (39-Zumar 3)

"When God, the One and Only is mentioned, the heart of those who believe not in the Hereafter are filled with disgust and horror, but when gods other than He are mentioned, behold they are filled with joy". Say, "O God, Creator of the Heavens and the earth. Knower of all that is hidden and open. It is thou that will judge between thy servants in those matters about which they have differed". "Even if the wrong-doers had all that there is on earth and as much more, in vain would they offer it for ransom from the pain of the Penalty on the Day of Judgement, But something will confront them from God, which they could never have counted upon. For the evils of their Deeds will confront them and they will be completely excluded by that which they used to mock at". (39 Zumar 45-48)

Say "Is it someone other than God that ye order me to worship, O ye ignorant ones". "But it has already been revealed to thee, as it was to those before thee". If thou wert to join gods with God, truly fruitless will be thy work and thou wilt surely be in the rank of those who lose, "Nay, but worship God and be those who give thanks". (39 Zumar 64-66)

"And we have indeed made the Quran easy to understand and remember. Then is there any that will receive admonition?" (55 Qamar 32)

"Among His Signs are the Night and the Day, and the Sun and the Moon. Adore not the sun and the moon but adore God Who created them. It is Him that ye wish to serve". (41 Ha Mim-as-Sajda 37)

"And thus have We by our command, sent inspiration to thee. Thou knowest not before what was revelation and what was faith but We have made the Quran a Light;

Wherewith We guide such of Our servants as We will and verily thou dost guide to the straightway; the way of God to Whom belongs whatever is in the heavens and whatever is on earth. Behold, how all affairs tend towards God". (41 Shura 52-53)

"Verily God will admit those who believe and do righteous deeds to Gardens, beneath which rivers flow; while those who reject God will enjoy this world and eat as cattle eat and the Fire will be their abode". (47 Muhammad 12)

3.45 **Peaceful Coexistence — Live and let live**

Say, "O ye that reject Faith. I worship not that which ye worship, nor will ye worship that which I worship. And I will not worship that which ye are wont to worship, nor will ye worship that which I worship. To you be your Way and to me mine". (109 Kafirúm 1-6)

"When comes the help of God and victory and thou dost see the people enter God's Religion in crowds, celebrate the praises of the Lord and pray for His Forgiveness; for He is Oft-Forgiving in Grace and Mercy". (110 Al-Nasr 1-3)

3.46 **The two kinds of verses in the Holy Quran**

"Nothing in the Earth or in the heavens is hidden from Allah. It is He who shapes you in the wombs of your mother as He wills. There is no deity but He, the Almighty, the Alwise. It is He who has sent down this Book to you. There are two kinds of verses in this book. Muhkamat[8] (which are precised in meaning). They are the essence of the book, and the other kind is Mutashabihat (which are ambiguous)".

3.47 "Muhkamat" is that which is precise, exact, clear and divisive. Muhkamat are those verses of the Quran which have been so couched as to make their meaning quite plain without any shade of ambiguity. They have been purposely so worded as to make their meaning definite and precise leaving little room for misinterpretation.

8. Maudoodi, Syed Abul Ala, *op. cit.* p. 215.

These verses constitute the fundamental principle of the Book, i.e., they and they alone determine the aim and object for which the Quran has been sent down. They invite the world to Islam, teach morals and give warnings. They refute wrong beliefs and practices, and lay down the way of right living. They expound the fundamentals of religion and State beliefs and practices, morals and duties, commandments and prohibitions. Therefore a seeker after Truth should turn to these verses as they alone can satisfy his needs. Naturally such a person will concentrate on these verses and endeavour to derive the greatest benefit from them.

3.48 "Mutashabihat" are those verses in which there is possibility of more than one meaning. Their object is to give a certain minimum knowledge about the universe, its beginning and end, the position of man therein, and such other basic things, for these things are essential for the formulation of any system of life. It is obvious that no human language possesses words, expressions, idioms etc. to depict clearly those supernatural things, which have never been grasped by human senses, nor seen, nor heard, nor smelt, nor touched, nor tested by human senses. That is why such supernatural things have to be described in terms of human life. That is why the Quran uses ambiguous or allegorical verses in human language which is liable give rise to more than one meaning. Thus it is clear that the main benefit of such verses is that they help to approach the Reality and form a conception of it. Hence the more one tries to determine their precise meanings, the more one gets involved in doubts and ambiguities. As a result of this one will not be able to find the Reality but will be led further away from it and cause mischief.

Therefore those, who seek after the Truth and do not hanker after superfluities, rest content with the simple idea of Reality they get from the ambiguous verses, which suffices them for an understanding of the Quran: they concentrate their whole attention on a fuller comprehension of the verses which are precise in meaning. On the other hand, those who love superfluities or seek after mischief, spend their time and energies in giving arbitrary interpretations to the ambiguous verses.

This might give rise to a question: how can one believe in the truth of the ambiguous verses, if one does not know their precise meaning? The answer is that a study of the precise verses, and not of the different interpretations of the ambiguous verses confirms a sensible man in his belief that the Quran is the World of Allah. When the study of the precise verses once convinces him that the Book is really from Allah, then the ambiguous verses do not create any doubt in his mind and he accepts the simple meanings which are within his comprehension and leaves alone any complicacies if and when they appear. Instead of hair splitting and probing into them, he believes in the Words of Allah as a whole and turns his attention to more useful things.

If must also be borne in mind that 'mutashabihat' are not ambiguous in themselves. They appear to be so only to our mind and we can claim to comprehend fully what is being conveyed to us. A better comprehension of the meaning of these verses is possible only when make attempt to understand them with utmost sincerity and profound devotion. It must also be fully understand that there is a complete coherence in all the verses of the Quran and that one does not come across any contradiction anywhere.

4

THE ISLAMIC FAITH

4.1 The meaning

The term Islam has been derived from the Arabic word 'Silm' meaning Peace, Tranquillity, Love and Shanti. It devises the solution of human problems so that mankind achieves real peace that otherwise has been eluding his grasp.

4.2 The present day world and the necessity of peace

The present day world with its unimaginable progress in its scientific discoveries and inventions for the comfort, and ease of life including (ROBOT)[1] available in Japan, America and other parts of Europe; but the peace is far off to reach the modern world. The World Assembly of the United Nations Organisation is keen and serious to devise ways and means to bring about peace in this world of prosperity and affluence but to no significant effect. Marx with his Das Capital and Feud with his Theory of Psychoanalysis and a host of other thinkers and sciéntists have not been able to unravel the mystery of peace with the result that mankind has become subject to stress of both mind and muscle, despite the affluence and prosperity brought about by the modern science. The biggest farm keepers, the richest industrialists, the most eminent

1. Machine like person.

scientists, the highest intellectuals, the Nobel Laureates, the investigators, researchers evidently appear to be baffled and non-plussed to find out the desired peace in spite of their best, continued and concentrated efforts. The Indian Sages and Rishis, no doubt, practised to obtain peace through their meditation and devotion to Supreme Power of the universe. Peace is of dire necessity for human life. Without peace life is miserable, torturous and not worth living.

4.3 Norms of the exchange of wishes among Muslims

When a Muslim meets another Muslim he at once wishes him "Assala-mo-Alaikum" (be peace of Allah on you). The other who is being saluted at once returns "Wa-alaikumus-Salam" (be peace of Allah on you also). A deep faith of Muslim is that peace is bestowed upon man by Allah or God, or the Supreme Power that guides the destiny of mankind. *This form of exchange of "Wishes" hammers the spirit of peace in the psyche of man in order to practise it in his day-to-day dealings with his family members, with his neighbours and with the society in which he lives.* It also indicates a Muslim's eternal quest for peace which he seeks and prays for.

4.4 Islam defined

An implicit Faith in the Invisible God, the Almighty, the righteous Actions (Amal), an entire submission and surrender to God and doing good to every body without any distinction of religion, creed, nationality and colour are the true definition of Islam as per admonitions of the Holy Quran and sayings (Hadith) of the Holy Prophet. The teachings of Islam are thus motivated at giving us the guidance to imbibe in us the virtues of love and affection, sympathy and kindness, equality, brotherhood and universal fraternity.

4.5 Origin

Islam is a very old religion as old as the creation of the world itself. No doubt Islam is the religion of all messengers and apostles who were sent to the world from time-to-time to reform and reclaim the people who fell off the righteous path and fell into depravity, degeneration and vices. Thus Islam has been coming from Adam to Noah, from Noah to Abraham and from Abraham to David, Moses and Jesus and lastly to Prophet Mohammad (be peace of Allah on him) of Arabia, who was the last Prophet of God and after him no Prophet is destined to come to the world. Islamic teachings thus started from Adam and ended and was completed with Hazrat Mohammad (be peace on him), with whom Prophethood was terminated.

4.6 **History**

Islam in the present form has been in existence since the revelation of the Holy Quran to the Prophet Mohammad (be peace of Allah on him). Of course, the basic teachings of the unity of God, piety of life doing good deeds are the same as found in those religions before the Holy Prophet, Mohammad (be peace of Allah on him). The Quran is the basic as well as the final constitution of an Islamic society which lays the basis of change in changing situations.

4.7 **Fundamentals**

The Fundamentals of Islam consist basically in two articles (1) Faith in the Invisibility (Imam bilghaib), (2) Action (Amal). Thus the Faith and the Action are the two inseparable articles in the Constitution of Islam.

4.8 **Faith defined**

Faith in the Invisibility of God, faith in the oneness of God, faith in angles, in His Prophets, in His Books, in the Day of Judgement and the faith in the accountability of good and bad actions are the essentials of the Faith. Faith gives us rationality in our thinking, willing and doing. Realising the importance of faith a famous philosopher of the west had to declare that — "the ages of faith are the ages of rationalism."[2] Thus faith is considered most

2. Quoted by Mohammad Iqbal in 'Six Lectures on the Reconstruction of Religious Thoughts in Islam', Lahore: Kapur Printing Works, 1930, p. 20.

significant part of human life. It gives us clear and positive thinking in our mind. It does not create doubt, misgivings, confusion and entangles us in the labyrinth of skepticism that deter us, as a matter of fact, to do things in a right and in rational way.

Faith is a force, a strength, a vitality, a dynamic and a grind stone to sharpen, to elevate, to develop the soul or spirit to the highest level, so as to acquire the knowledge of the Supreme Powers of God, the Almighty, His Omnipotence, His Omniscience and His Omnipresence.

4.9 Actions (Amal)

Actions consist of observing four practices:

(1) Prayer (Namaz) (2) Fasting (Roza) (3) Payments of poor rates (Zakat) (4) Pilgrimage (Haj)

4.10 Prayer (Salat)[3]

The salat is obligatory upon every Muslim male and female who has attained the age of discretion. It is offered five times a day.

"All those who believe in God are knit together by prayers for which they must congregate five times a day".

"And bow down their heads with those who bow down in worship". (The Holy Quran 2.43)

4.11 Timings of prayers

1. 'Salat-ul-Fijre', the morning prayer which is said after dawn and before sunrise.
2. 'Dhuhr' (Zoher) in the early afternoon when the sun begins to decline and its time extends the time of Asr.

3. The Holy Quran says "Recite that which has been revealed to you of the Book and that keep us prayer, surely keep you away from indecency and evil and certainly the remembrance of Allah is the Greatest". (29.45) Prayer should be sincere and not degenerating into a mere ritual, into a lifeless and a rapid ceremony; such prayer is denounced by the Holy Quran : "Woe to the praying ones who are unmindful of their prayers." (107.5)

3. 'Asr' prayer is offered in the late afternoon when the sun is midway to its course to setting and its time extends a little before Magherib prayer.
4. 'Magherib' or the sun-set prayer is offered immediately after the sunset.
5. 'Isha', or the early night prayer is said when the red glow in the western horizon disappears and its time extends to midnight. But it must be said before retiring.

Note : The service of the Friday takes the place early afternoon prayer ('Dhuhr').

4.12 **Prepration for the prayers**

Before offering each prayer one has to be neat and clean. If he is unclean, he must take bath and cleanse himself before he offers prayer. Neatness and cleanliness are essentially important. Neatness and cleanliness are the integral part of the practice.

4.13 **Ablution ('Wudu')**[4]

Before saying prayers it is essentially necessary to wash those parts of the body which are generally exposed. The ablution is performed thus:

1. The hands are cleansed washing up to wrists;
2. Then the mouth is cleansed with a tooth-brush, fresh twigs or simply with water;
3. Then the nose is cleansed with the nostrids with water;
4. Then the face is washed;
5. Then the right arm and left arm are washed up to the elbow;

4. (a) A fresh ablution is necessary only when a person has attended the call of nature or has been asleep.
   (b) When a person is sick, weak, old and infirm and water is not within reach 'Tayammum' is allowed in its place of ablution.

   'Tayammum' is performed by touch of pure earth with both hands, and then wipe over the face with this only once, and then the backs of the two hands.

6. The head is then wiped over with wet hands, the three fingers and thumb of both hands being joined together; and
7. The feet are then washed up to the ankles, the right foot first and the left after.

But if there are sick on, and they have been put on after performing an ablution, it is not necessary to take them off: the wet hands may be passed over them. It is, however, necessary that the socks be taken off and the feet washed about once in every twenty-four hours.

4.14 Sincerity in prayer (Salat)

Prayer should not be the only recitation with the tongue without understanding and reflecting on the meaning of the words uttered with the result they fail to set in action those thought processes which are most essential to bring about a real change in men, a change in his thinking, a change in his doing that develops distinct personality of his own with sincerity, sublimity, honesty, and integrity with love for truth and respect for humanity with no air of superiority over his fellow men for his wealth and power but truly humble, trust-worthy and co-operative out and out in every aspect of life Here and chosen one Hereafter.

4.15 Fasting ('Saum')

Fasting is the second important part of Action or 'Amal'. The number of days on which fasts are to be observed is twenty nine or thirty according to the number of days of the month of 'Ramadan' depending upon the visibility of the moon. Food and drink are prohibited on the fast days from dawn to sunset. So also a sexual intercourse. The fasting month (The Ramadan) being a lunar month, falls in different seasons in different years and accordingly days are longer and shorter. Fasting does not mean simply abstaining from food, and drink but from every kind of evil. A man is allowed not to keep fast if he is sick or on travel. Similarly a woman who is in the family way or gives such is also free not to keep fast but they must keep fast for such days when they are well and fit. Persons who are constantly ill or because of their old age and infirmity cannot bear the hardship of keeping fast are excused, but they should give away a poor man's food every day within their means.

As regards Fasting God says in the Holy Quran:

> "O Ye who believe fasting is prescribed for you just as it was prescribed for those before you so that you may learn self-restraint fasting for a fixed number of days. But if any of you is ill or on a journey, the prescribed number should be made up from days later and for those who find hard to do so there is a ransom, the feeding of one who is indigent. But he that will give more out of his own free will it is better for him. And it is better for you that ye fast, if ye only knew." (2 : 183-184)

4.16 **Poor rate (the 'Zakat')**

The payment of poor rate or Zakat is obligatory and binding upon every Muslim. The Zakat, according to the saying of the Holy Prophet is a charitable Gift taken from the rich for the benefit of the poor. Payment of poor rate is an act of 'Shariah' out of the annual savings of every Muslim. It has to be taken out and compulsorily set apart for the use as indicated in para 4.17 below:

As for the 'Zakat', God says in the Holy Quran:

> "By no means shall ye attain righteousness, unless ye give freely of that which ye love and whatever ye give of a truth God Knoweth it well." (3 : 92)

4.17 **Payment of Zakat**

The payment of Zakat is scheduled to be made on the following heads as mentioned in the Holy Quran.[6]

1. The poor
2. The needy
3. Those in debt
4. (Ransoming) of captives

6. The Holy Quran (9 : 60).

5. The way-farer
6. The officials appointed in connection with collection and expenditure of Zakat
7. Those whose hearts are made to incline to truth
8. The way of Allah.

This indicates emergence of a system of corporate and collective collection and disbursement of Zakat rather than by individuals.

4.18 **Pilgrimage or ('Hajj')**

Performance of pilgrimage to Mecca is incumbent upon every Muslim once in his life, subject to the condition that he has the means to undertake the journey as well as to make the provision for those dependents on him. The pilgrimage is performed in the month of Zilhaj. As regards the formalities to be observed during the pilgrimage every one can easily learn them from 'Muallim', or instructor.

4.19 **The 'Arkan' or principal points**

The Arkan or the principal points in connection with the pilgrimage are:

1. Entering upon the State of Ihram in which the ordinary clothes are put off and all pilgrims wear one kind of apparel consisting of two seamless wrappers and head uncovered.
2. Twaf, or making circuits round the Ka'ba seven times.
3. Sa'y, or running seven times between Safa and Marwa two small hills.
4. Staying in the 'plain of Arafat'.

4.20 **Significance of Ihram (seamless wrapper)**

This state of Ihram makes all men and all women stand upon one place of equality all wearing the simple dress and living in the same conditions. All distinctions of rank and colour, of wealth and nationality disappear there, and the King is there indistinguishable from the peasant. The whole of humanity assumes one aspect on attitude before its Maker, and then the grandest and the noblest sight of human equality is witnessed in the wonderful desert plain called the 'Arafat', which truly enables a man to have a true knowledge of his Creator, the word being derived from 'Arafat' meaning he came to have a knowledge (of the thing). It must be admitted that the whole of the world is unable to present another such noble picture of real brotherhood, and practical equality.

4.21 Benefits of the four Actions (Amal)

The benefits of the Four Actions (Amal) to man are many; a few of them are indicated below:

A. Personal hygiene: neatness and cleanliness of the person, of the environment and of the regime tends to create a healthy atmosphere in the family and to ward off many infections of diseases.

B. Formation of the habit of early rising
To say the morning prayer man has to get up early in the morning. The benefit of early rising is best explained in the off-quoted epigram of the English language, "Early to bed and early to rise makes a man healthy, wealthy and wise". This shows that early rising is universally recognised.

C. Sort of physical exercise
In order to say the morning prayer one has to walk a distance up to mosque of the locality and thus he has an access to physical exercise by walking as well by the prescribed movements during the prayer. It is enjoined upon every body to say his prayers in the mosque with other inhabitant of the locality.

D. Habit of electing a leader
In order to lead the prayer a leader or Imam is indispensable. The Imam must be fully qualified with good and honest character. He must be trustworthy with all the good qualities of a Imam. He must be a fair or he or she be fully conversant with the correct recitation of the

Holy Quran. Imam is rather a permanent body in the mosque or is elected for among the inhabitants of the locality with these qualities as referred to above.

E. Habit of obeying the leader is formed which is of dire necessity in the democratic set of life.

F. Co-operation

The offering of prayer together with the same disciplined movements instils the habit of working together and thus enable us to adopt a life of co-operative and working together in every field of activities

G. Habit of devotion and concentration

Prayers enable us to form the habit of devotion and concentration in the discharge of our duties, and doing the work assigned to us most devotedly and efficiently

H. Consciousness of social adjustment

After prayer in the mosque we may have social contact with the persons assembled and exchange of views on matters relating to social problems, and solutions by helping each other in time of distress and need. In this way we are acquainted with the different social problems of the locality and find out their solution in co-operation with each other. In this way our social outlook is greatly increased for the work of social life in the wider field of activities be local, regional, national or international.

I. Habit of punctuality

Habit of punctuality is created, that is to do all work in time and, as a matter of fact the habit of punctuality is of great importance in every walk of life. All thinkers and educationists have laid stress on the importance of punctuality as it is the potent factor in the building of character of man. Without the habit and practice of punctuality he is apt to meet failure in his life.

4.22 **Benefits of Fasting (Saum)**

The benefits of fasting are many but a few of them are enumerated here for the knowledge of the readers. Man is enjoined to keep himself away from such bad habits as drinking of alcohol and other substance of intoxication including drugs, telling a lie, speaking ill of others in their absence, using abusive and filthy language, stealing of the things of others, looking at the face of other man's wife or commit adultery or whoredom, robbery, kidnapping, hijacking, violence, bloodshed and terrorism. But during fasting he is to keep himself busy with the remembrance of God, recitation of Holy Quran inviting the guests, friends, wayfarers to the repast at the time of breaking fast, giving food and alms to the poor. He is to attend the special prayer in which the Holy Quran is recited by a Hafiz[7] for about two hours in the night before retiring to bed. This sort of constant and regular practice in the most disciplined manner will surely enable one to do good things and to shun evil and bad things, and to walk on the righteous path and to avoid going on the wrong and prohibited path, and in this way he develops all the best traits of character and thus he builds his own personality and individuality to become an agreeable member of the society, a dutiful and conscious citizen of the state and an asset to the entire humanity.

4.23 **Payment of Zakat (Poor Tax or Poor Dues)**

Payment of poor tax as indicated in para 4.17 is also helpful in solving the problems of the society where rich and poor live side by side. The rich have riches, affluences and wealth to lead a happy life of ease and comfort while the poor are destitute and hang on a life of poverty, of wants, of needs, of afflictions, of diseases and of terrors and thus the payment of poor rate or the poor dues is the best source of relief to that segment of the downtrodden society. Here it must be borne in mind that this amount of Zakat is to be taken as due from the rich to the poor.

7. Hafiz is one who learns the whole Quran by rote.

According to Islamic belief it is not an act of bounty or a benevolence but it is a due to be paid compulsorily to the poor as taxes are paid to the state. In this way the "rich will not be richer and poor will not be poorer", and thus the doctrine of Zakat is a key to the solution of the problem of inequality in the distribution of wealth with no class-war, no class conflict, with no class hatred, with no violence and bloodshed between the bourgeois and the proletariat and thus the establishment of socialism in the policy of economy is visualised as per admonition and commandment of the Holy Quran.

4.24 **'Hajj', the pilgrimage**

This practice of Hajj has manifold benefits besides bestowing peace and tranquillity in performing the obligation according to the wishes of God, the Almighty, man learns many new things, obtains various experiences during the travel to Mecca, He comes into contact with people of different countries with different languages, of different colour and thus he acquaints himself with their way of life, their manners and customs, their social problems, their system of education, their trades and occupations and thus the social contacts of this kind broaden the outlook and widen the mental horizon of man, and in this way he is fully equipped for the adjustment in the society in which he lives with an attitude of co-operation and mutual help and trust. The occasion of haj is also an opportunity to collectively deliberate and evolve the solution of the problems that may confront the Umma.

4.25 **The real training of man**

According to the Holy Quran Man is the vicegerent of God, the Almighty on the earth. God, therefore, wants to see him as perfect as possible in all aspect of life. Through the prescribed actions and implicit Faith in the Invisible God, the training of Man is being conducted as referred to in the foregoing paragraphs. Man has, therefore, the obligation to fulfil as enjoined upon him. (He is answerable for all his actions good or bad before God, and the records of actions in this world are duly kept. The Holy Quran says: "And who so doeth good an atom's weight shall see it then and whose doeth ill an atom's weight shall see it then." (the Holy Quran, 99 : 7-8)

And thus the man becomes conscious of his responsibilities and duties and does his work in a righteous way with a fear of the Unseen; in this way his traits, character and personality are built; and he becomes a perfect man, peace loving, dutiful, responsible, conscientious with a high sense of morality, justice, equity, self-sacrifice, devotion and services to his society, to his own country and to the world at large.

4.26 An Accord between Matter and Spirit

No doubt the present day world is highly industrial, urbanized and civilized so far as materialism is concerned but basically it lacks awefully in spiritualism with the result that, despite the progress and affluence, there is tension, apprehension, fear, restlessness, frustration and want of mutual trust and confidence because of a vacuum between Matter and Spirit. The vacuum can only be removed by having faith in the Invisible God — the Maker, the Cherisher and the Sustainer and by the action of righteousness; thus there will be an accord between Matter and Spirit. As a matter of fact, Matter and Spirit are interdependent and are inseparable. A harmonious blending between the two is absolutely necessary for the world to usher in to a new era of peace, prosperity, health and happiness for all times to come.

5

THE QURAN AND THE CONTEMPORARY CHALLENGES

5.1 The present age

The present age is an age of materialism, an age of atom, an age of computers and mastery over space, an age of scientific inventions and discoveries, an age of cancers and AIDS, an age of disease and pestilence, an age of famines and drought, an age of intoxicants and drugs, an age of sexual imbalance and pornography, an age of biological transgression and perversity, an age of violence and terrorism, an age of hijacking and highway robbery, an age of fatal accidents in the space and below the space, an age of strikes and bandh, an age of slogans and fast unto death, an age of family breakups, and social maladjustments, an age of delinquency and perversion, an age of affluence and poverty, an age of psychosis and psychoneurosis, an age of fear and suspense, an age of stress and strain and above all an age of nuclear arsenals and star wars.

5.2 Man is himself responsible for such state of affairs

No doubt man has progressed materially with great speed and rapidity — but with the same rapidity and speed he has deteriorated spiritually. His socialisation, his education, his environment, his way of life, his mode of thinking, his manner of doing are all out-an-out materialistic devoid of spiritualism. Of course he has wrought wonders in the achievement of material progress but he has wilfully ignored the spiritual significance with the result that the world has degenerated into disorder, depravity, maladies and afflictions. The matter and spirit should have been harmonized for the real progress of mankind. The spirit can only be developed with implicit faith in the Invisible Supreme Power God the Almighty and in His Divine Law for the regulation, governance and control and conduct of human life to avoid human maladies and afflictions.

5.3 Modern civilization and maladies

Surgeon Hastings Gilford[1] has rightly said in his book "Tumors and Cancers" that "Civilization provides environment favourable to the growth of degenerative disorders including cancer." And no doubt there are a number of fatal and dreadful diseases like AIDS that has been a challenge to the medical world. If things go on as they do there is no wonder that many more diseases may emerge to afflict mankind.

5.4 Diseases in groups

According to the same Surgeon,[2] when we regard diseases, as it were from a distance, so as to observe their place in nature and their relations one to another and to normal processes, we can but notice that they are naturally arranged in groups. These groups are not the groups we are accustomed to see in text books, such as are founded upon anatomical grounds, but are based firstly on their nature, secondly on causes.

1. Gilford, Hastings, 'Tumors and Cancers' with an introduction by Sir F. Rederick, London, H.K. Lewis & Co. Ltd, 1925, p. 388.
2. *Ibid.* p. 436.

5.5 Sexual-filth diseases

We can, thus, readily distinguish an order or group of sexual-filth diseases with syphilis and gonorrhoea at its heads, containing in its ranks such as well known disorders, as salpingitis, pelvis abcess, cystitis, sterility, ophthalmia, arthritis, tabes, general paralysis, alcoholism. Such are the maladies which naturally be expected by any medical scientist in venereal clinic or hospital. Corresponding social disorders are poverty, vice and crime.

5.6 Deficiency disease class

There is a deficiency disease class with rickets, scurvy and beri-beri as its leaders comprising diarrhoea, anaemia, mal-nutrition, bodily deformities, tuberculosis, as correlated diseases.

5.7 Filthy air group

Another important group is that of filthy air with tuberculosis at the head. It includes mal-nutrition, anaemia, malformations.

5.8 Alcoholic group

Alcoholism leads the band of which drunkenness, amentia, dementia, insanity, crime, cocainism, morphinism, gonorrhoea, syphilis and other vices are important members.

5.9 The filthy food group

The filthy food group consists of enteric fever standing conspicuously from other disorders which come from dirty food and drink, such as enteritis, and other forms of intestinal poisoning, malnutrition, cholera, diarrhoea, tuberculosis.

5.10 Cancer and AIDS are the outstanding

Now we are able after the same fashion to reorganise a large and important group of disorders, of which the chief outstanding members are cancers and AIDS. In this great array of diseases, are the tumors, malformations, amentia, dementia, insanity, neuroses, psychoses in general, alcoholism, syphilis, gonorrhoea, diabetes, sterility. All of these and more, we have seen to be the disorders of the materialistic civilization.

5.11 The guidance of the Quran

The Quran has given us a number of warnings to eschew from such evil practices as are responsible for the maladies and afflictions of the present civilization and at the same time has taught us a number of measures for the prevention and control of such fatal diseases as referred to above. In this respect Quran has also cited examples of those former tribes, clans and people who were severely punished for going astray from the right path and for wishfully neglecting the Divine laws and resorting to injustice as dealt with in the preceding paragraphs of the book.

5.12 The necessity of the Quran is universally recognised

In view of the fact that the Quran comprises of a varied variety of knowledge, be of medical science, social science, political science, and sciences of Law and Justice; and there are many scientific truths contained in it and as such the revealed truth gives clues for solving what are today the most intractable problems facing the world; the Quran covers all sciences in general but not specifically; the Quran is undoubtedly always right while human theories and hypotheses are not perfect and may be altered or disproved. The truth of the interpretation of Holy Text on which discoveries are based are now accepted and recognised wholly or partially.

5.13 An excerpt from the writing of Sir Edward Denison Ross[3] recognising the necessity of the Quran is given below :

3. See p. VII by Sir Edward Denison Ross in his introduction of the Koran translated by George Sale.

"through all the vicissitudes of thirteen hundred years the Koran has remained the sacred book of all the Turks and Persians and of nearly quarter of the population of India. Surely such a book as deserves to be widely read in the West, more specially in these days when space and time have been almost annihilated by modern invention and when public interest embraces the whole world."

5.14 Prevention and prohibition of sexual-filth diseases under the Quranic injunction

During the recent years round about 1980 the medical world witnessed with much horror the emergence of AIDS (Acquired Immuno Deficiency Syndrome) which has been creating a havoc on the entire globe mostly in the USA and in the west with a heavy toll of the millions of human life particularly of youngmen who died miserable death of pains and agony with no suitable drugs or vaccine available for their succour and relief. This detestable and abominable disease is the consequence of sexual perversity, homosexuality, sodomy or anal sex — a clear biological transgression for which severe warnings were given to the people of lot to desist from such vice as per injunction contained in the verses of the Quran duly quoted in the preceding paras of this book. Severe punishments were given by destroying them. The symbol of their destruction still stands as deterrent for the sinners. The havoc of this dreaded disease can very well be imagined by the latest report on "AIDS on Increase" by World Health Organisation (WHO) as reported in the Daily Hindustan Times, Patna, 6th September 1988 which is given below:

"AIDS on Increase"

New Delhi. Sept. 5 - The World Health Organisation (WHO) has said that the number of reported cases of AIDS and countries reporting AIDS have continued to increase. As of August one, 1988, over 108,000 AIDS cases have been officially reported by 140 countries. However, this number represents only a portion of the total cases of AIDS to date, which are estimated at approximately 200,000 to 250,000.

WHO estimates that between five and ten million persons may be currently infected with human immuno-deficiency virus (HIV) — the virus which causes AIDS.

The largest number of cases (nearly 80,000) have been reported from 40 countries and territories and the Americas. Nearly 70,000 cases have been reported in the United States, where the disease was first recognised in 1981.

In 39 other countries in the Americas, nearly 10,000 cases have been reported. In the Americas, Europe, Australia and New Zealand, most AIDS cases occur among homosexuals or bisexuals men and intravenous drug users between the ages of 20 and 49. The proportion of cases acquired through heterosexual contact in these areas is estimated at about five percent.

In Europe, 28 countries have reported over 13,000 AIDS cases.

5.15 **Chinese notion about AIDS**[4]

The Chinese call "AIDS God's visitation on the human race for their unpardonably frivolous approach to **sex**" and they further say that "the Chinese nurtured by their traditional culture and moral values, adopt a much more serious attitude towards sexual behaviour than in the west and there is far less sexual misbehaviour. It is no accident that a great nation that often claims her people enjoy the greatest freedom in the world is the very nation that now has the greatest number of AIDS patient." According to conservative estimates, more than 120,000 AIDS cases have been registered in 142 countries around the world with an additional five to ten million of people carrying the virus. By 1991, a million more people around the world will have contracted the dreaded disease.

5.16 **Heterosexuality (fornication and adultery)**

Heterosexuality is another evil of modern perverted civilization that causes AIDS and venereal diseases, gonorrhoea and syphilis and other sexually transmitted disease (STDS) fully discussed in para 5.5 of this chapter.

4. News item published in the Hindustan Times, Patna dated 9 December 1988.

5.17 Venereal disease (syphilis and gonorrhoea)

Syphilis is a highly poisonous infection, which is acquired by co-habitation with the woman who has already had the disease including prostitutes. It is also acquired by inheritance from parents, who might have had it either by direct acquirement or by inheritance in their turn. Syphilis appears in the shape of ulceration inflammation on the glands which is identified as cancer. It is at first a manifestation on the sexual organs. Then the disease is carried through whole organism by means of lymphatic system, and affect particularly subcutaneous and submucous cellular tissues, the fibrous osseous and cartilagenous tissues and lastly the whole constitution of man with bone diseases, gammata or soft tumour like growth in the deeper tissues including cancers. Ulceration of genital lesions may enhance transmission of HIV perhaps by providing a more direct portal of entry into blood stream.

5.18 Venereal disease sycosis (gonorrhoea)

Sycosis (Gonorrhoea) is also highly poisonous infection which is acquired by co-habitation with a woman who has already had it including prostitutes. It is also acquired by inheritance. Gonorrhoea shows itself by an ulceration and inflammation in the canal and also in the root of the genital organ with a sloughy discharge; the penis is more or less indurated attended with swelling of the lymphatic glands on its dorsus. Figwarts grow about the genital and anus at the juncture of the external skin with mucous membranes, appear like cauliflowers. They are dry or exude a slimy, acrid, badly swelling and contagious fluids.

5.19 Prostitutes and AIDS[5]

Prostitutes and other groups of women identified as prostitutes are reservoir of AIDS and sexually transmitted diseases (STDS) including Syphilis and Gonorrhoea. The prostitutes are the group of the high risk for becoming infected with human immuno deficiency virus (HIV) and for other STDS.

5. See page 418 American Journal of Public Health, April 1988.

5.20 Lot's people committed homosexuality and were destroyed

In Quran, God said "And (we sent) Lot when he said to his people : Most surely you are guilty of an indecency which none of the nations has ever done before you."

"What ! do you come to the males and commit robbery on the highway, and you commit evil deeds in your assemblies ? But nothing was the answer of his people except they said : Bring on us Allah's chastisement, if you are one of the faithful. He said : My Lord ! help me against the mischievous people."

"Surely we will cause to come down upon the people of this town[6] a punishment from heaven because they transgressed."

"And certainly we have left a clear sign of it for a people who understand."[7] (Quran 29 : 28-29, 30-34-35)

5.21 Punishment of God

"So each We punished for his sin : and of them was he on whom we sent down a violent storm, and of them was he whom the rumbling overtook, and of them was he whom We made to be swallowed up by the earth, and of them was he whom we drowned, and it did not beseem Allah that He should be unjust to them, but they were unjust to their own souls." (Quran 29 : 40)

5.22 Homosexuality and punishment

"What do you come to the males from among creatures?"

"And leave what has been created for you of your wives? nay, you are a people exceeding limits."

"They said: If you desist not, O Lot you shall surely be those who are expelled."

6. Sodom and Gomorrah, the cities destroyed, are in the neighbourhood of the Dead Sea, on the road from Arabia, and surely it is on a road that still abides.
7. The whole tract on the east side of the Dead Sea (where the cities were situated) is covered with Sulphurous Salts and is deadly to animal and plant life. It is the scene of utter destruction that should stand as a symbol of Destruction that awaits sin. (P. 1037), The Holy Quran Text, Translation and Commentary by A. Yusuf Ali.

"He said : Surely I am of those who utterly abhor your doing."

"Then we utterly destroyed the others."

"And we rained down upon them a rain, and evil was the rain on those warned."

"Most surely there is a sign in this but most of them do not believe."[8]

8. It is in the fitness of things to observe here that homosexuality, sodomy or anal sex between males is the most heinous sinful crime before God, The Almighty and for this people of Lot were punished and the entire city of Sodom and the adjoining cities were destroyed by storms, rains and earthquake. The truth of the saying of the Quran is duly corroborated by other reliable sources of the present day research. (See pages 285-286 of The Universal Bible Dictionary, John Macpherson, Published by Hodder and Stoughton, 1892).
"Sodom an important city in the fruitful valley of Seedim, being first among the five, which beside it were Gomorrah, Admah, Zeboim and Bela or Zoar. Lot was tempted by the uncommonly rich soil and general fertility of the district to choose the valley in which Sodom lay, to pitch his tent near Sodom and ultimately to take up his residence within the city. Their territory indeed lay outside of what is ranked as Canaan, but the inhabitants, though never called Cannanites, most probably belonged to the race, and has become morally degraded to a terrible degree. Each town in federation had its own king, but all combined to repel the attack of an enemy under the Leadership of the King of Sodom. The city lay in what is now the extreme southern part of the Dead Sea. That some catastrophe, like that recorded in Genxix caused the destruction of the cities of the plain, may be accepted as a historical fact, of which we have a report in Strabo and even Tacitus. The biblical writer as well as early travellers like Burchhardt assume that previous to this occurrence the Jordan flowed through the valley to the Flanitic Gulf. Such a change as led to the formation of the Dead Sea must be quite prehistoric, and the local convulsion which destroyed the cities can only be deepened as sea already existing. The Israelites always regarded the overthrow of Sodom as a terrible warning of the doom of defiant ungodliness.

"And most surely your Lord is the Mighty, the Merciful". (Quran 26 : 165-166-167-168, 172-173-174-175)

5.23 The Quranic injunction for the prohibition of sexual imbalance

The Quran has taken a number of measures for prohibiting sexual imbalance and sexual waywardness including fornication and adultery.

The Quran enjoins upon men to regulate and control sex as the sexual indecency and sexual ills are the root cause of many human maladies and miseries as pointed out in the foregoing para 5.5 of this book. The following verses of the Quran forbid homosexuality, fornication, adultery and whoredom.

(A) "And go not nigh to fornication; Surely it is an indecency and evil is the way." (17 : 32)

The Quran not only forbids fornication but enjoins men not only to go near it, thus avoiding all the opportunities which are likely to tempt one to fall into the evil.

(B) "Successful indeed are the believer who guard their private parts". "Except before their mates or those who their right hands possess for they surely are not blameable".

(C) "But whoever seeks to go beyond that these are they that exceed the limit". (23 : 1, 5, 6, 7)

5.24 Prohibition of indecency in the society

Muslim man or woman is not allowed to expose, in the presence of others, any part of the body which it is not decent to expose but a certain degree of freedom is allowed to women in the presence of their husbands and female servants, and to men in the presence of their wives.

According to Islamic ideas of decency, the exposure of such parts of the body as European ladies are generally in the habit of exposing in ballroom and theatres is disallowed. The Islamic teachings are very particular in giving guidance to maintain decency in the relation of man and woman. Such sorts of indecency are the root cause of social evils. Therefore such habits are forbidden in the good of the human society. The Quran, as a matter of fact, enjoins upon every body to maintain a decent and healthy norm in the society and wipe out the evils of pornography and nakedness that are beyond doubt responsible for the evils and maladies in human life.

5.25 Preventive measures adopted by the Quran against the immoral relationship between men and women in the society

(A) "Say to the believing men that they cast down their looks and guard their private parts ; that is purer for them; Surely Allah is aware of what they do". (Quran 24 : 30)

(B) "And say to the believing women that they cast down their looks and guard their private parts and not display their ornaments except what appears thereof; and let them wear their head coverings over their bosoms, and not display their ornaments except to their husbands, or their fathers, or the fathers of their husbands, or their sons, or their sisters, or their sister's sons, or their women, or those whom their right hands possess, or the male servants not having need (of women), or the children who have not attained knowledge of what is hidden of women ; and let them not strike their feet so that what they hide of their ornaments may be known ; and turn to Allah of You, O believers ! so that you may be successful." (Quran 24 : 31)

(C) "And let those who do not find a match keep chaste until Allah makes them free from want out of His grace". (Quran 24 : 33)

5.26 The preventive measures most scientific and pragmatic

It admits of no doubt that the preventive measures adopted by the Quran are most decent and scientific and biologically quite in keeping with human nature. It regulates the relations between men and women and puts a check on a too-free intermingling of males and females. Both men and women are enjoined to cast down their looks, not to expose their private parts, and keep themselves away from the evils of fornication, adultery and promiscuity. The women are enjoined in particular to keep their ornaments concealed and not to display their decoration and dress as they are the cause of attracting the attention of males and as such a restraint is put. Further it is enjoined that a woman when going out should have herself covered over by an external wrapper or an overcoat, it being permissible to have the hands and the face uncovered. The exposure of such parts as the neck, the bosom, or the arms is forbidden and also the display of decoration whether in the form of ornaments or dress. This display of ornaments is allowed only before certain relatives and dependents mentioned in the verses above. Such guidance to women will indeed go a long way to check the evils of the society that are responsible for man's sufferings. This may be noticed how simple, practical, judicious and psychological is the guidance.

5.27 **Free mixing of men and women — a social evil**

No body can deny the fact that the free mixing of men and women in the modern society in public places, in the restaurants and clubs, in the offices, and in co-educational institutions, with no restraint rather with so-called freedom in the name of modernity and for equality with men, is solely responsible for heterosexuality, sexual perversity and promiscuity with the result that the society suffers from dreadful diseases like cancers and AIDS and other sexually transmitted diseases (STDS) — a source of human sufferings and afflictions. (Glory be to God the Almighty — Who has given a guidance to mankind through His Book to safeguard against such catastrophe and destruction. The Quran, the Book of Allah, revealed to the Holy Prophet, Mohammad (be peace of Allah on him) is the great blessing to mankind).

5.28 **Alcoholism**

It has been seen in para 5.8 of the book that alcoholism leads the band of which drunkenness, amentia, dementia, insanity, crime, cocainism, morphism, gonorrhoea, syphilis and other vices are important members; the un-imaginable use of alcohol and drugs in the present-day society is vastly responsible for the encouragement of sexual imbalances and other vices.

5.29 **Alcoholism made unlawful by the Quranic injunction**

(A) "They ask you about drinking and gambling, Say, There is great harm in both, though there is some benefit also for people. But the harm of the sin therefore is far greater than their benefit." (Quran 2 : 219)

(B) "O Believers ! do not offer Prayers while you are intoxicated, for Prayer should be offered only when you know what you are saying. Likewise do not offer Prayer, if you are "unclean" until you take your bath, except when passing on the way; and if you are sick or on a journey or if any one of you has relieved himself or you have touched women and can find no water; then cleanse yourselves with pure dust by rubbing it on your face and hands; no doubt Allah is Lenient and Forgiving." (Quran 4 : 43)

(C) "Believers, wine and games of chance, idols, divining arrows, are abominations devised by the devil. Avoid them, so that you may prosper. The devil seeks to stir up enmity and hatred among you by means of intoxicants and gamblings, and to keep you off from the remembrance of Allah and from your prayers. Will you not abstain from them ?" (Quran 5 : 90-91)

5.30 **Bad effects of alcoholism and drugs**

Under the influence of alcohol and drugs one loses all senses of morality and become, instantly a brute or a beast and stoops so low as to commit incest and co-habits with female members of his own family. Not satisfied sexually he runs to the houses of women of ill repute, prostitutes and whores and contacts venereal diseases like syphilis and gonorrhoea and then comes back to members of his own family and infects them with this highly poisonous infections and in this way the entire society is contaminated and thus a cycle of infections is set on moving without termination, from male to female and vice-versa. This sorrowful state of affairs is the major cause of all sorts of maladies, vices and evils.

5.31 **Drunkenness a major social problem**

Drunkenness has become a major social problem in Europe and America. Drunken drivers of motor cars, trucks, transport vehicles cause traffic accidents on the streets and roads thereby injure or kill other people and themselves get injured, maimed, imprisoned or killed. Besides accidents on the roads, there are in sea planes and mid air. This phenomenon of drunken driving and hazard of accidents of highways and roads has become a regular feature throughout the world including India.

According to an American finding of 8th July 1985,[9] the effects of alcoholism are very serious in United States and Central America. For instance, 50% of the people who die in traffic accidents in Puerto Rico are alcohol addicts. Similarly, all victims of suicide in Mexico have been found to possess alcohol in their blood. Moreover alcoholism creates vitamin disorder in human body causing deficiency of vitamin B-1. According to other sources, liquor drinking has caused absenteeism among workers in Western factories and industries. This has led to the decrease in productivity. The Western researchers have demonstrated that higher consumption is harmful to the body, and soul, character and behaviour of many individuals with personality disorders.

9. Quote Weekly Radiance, Delhi, 27th November-3rd December 1988.

5.32 **The filthy food group**[10]

The filthy food group consists of enteric fever standing conspicuously from other disorders which come from dirty food and drink, causing enteritis and other forms of intestinal poisoning, mal-nutrition, cholera, diarrhoea and tuberculosis.

5.33 **A clear guidance**

The Quran has given a clear guidance with emphasis on lawful and clean food.

(A) "O people, eat of what is lawful and clean in the earth and do not follow the ways of Satan for he is your avowed enemy. He enjoins you to comit vice and indecency and induces to attribute to Allah's name things you do not know to be from Him." (Quran 2 : 168-69)

(B) "O believers, if you are true worshippers of Allah alone eat without hesitation of the good and clean things wherewith we have provided you and be grateful to Allah, Allah has forbidden only these things; do not eat what dies of itself, nor blood, nor swineflesh, nor what has been consecrated to any other name than of Allah. But one will incur no sin if, forced by absolute necessity, he eats of any of these forbidden things, provided he has no intention of transgressing the law and does not take more than what is absolutely indispensable; for Allah is very Forgiving and Merciful." (Quran 2 : 172-173)

5.34 **The true guidance**

The above verses contain the injunction that only the lawful, pure, clean and good food should be eaten. The lawful things are not only those which the law has not declared to be forbidden, but even unforbidden things become unlawful if they are acquired unlawfully, e.g. by theft, robbery, cheating, bribery etc. The Quran recognises

10. See footnote nos. 1 and 2 of this chapter.

relation between the physical and the spiritual condition of man. It admits of no doubt that food plays an important role in the formation of character ; and the heart and the brain powers are obviously affected by the quality of food taken. As the Quran is meant for all stages of the development of human society it contains rules and regulations for the betterment of the physical as well as the moral and the spiritual conditions of man.

The injunction to eat of the good things is directed against the use of things which are injurious to health as well as against what is unlawfully acquired.

5.35 Avoid jealousy, backbiting and suspicion of each other

"Ye who believe ! Avoid suspicion as much (as possible); for suspicion in some cases are sin ; And spy not on each other, Nor speak ill of each other, Behind, their backs.

Would any of you like to eat,
The flesh of his dead
Brother ? Nay, you would
Abhor it, But fear God;
For God is of Returning
Most Merciful." (Quran 49 : 11-12)

The above verses deal with some of the evils which are most rampant in civilized societies, which corrupt the society to its core. These evils mostly arise with wealth, for living in ease, people are mostly concerned with seeking each other's faults and thus mutual hatred takes the place of brotherly love and family concord and thus there is mal-adjustment in the social order, besides disease and maladies. Modern research on the subject noted above enlightens that the fact of a person continually jealous over a period of years contorts and charges in expression, till it can look persistently evil, the glands secrete chemicals in the blood and eventually poison the system and produce stomach ulcer or even cancer. No emotion so warps the nature and destroys both mind and body.

5.36 **World as one human family**

Injunction for universal fraternity, equality and to consider world as one Human Family.

> "O you men ! Surely we have created you of a male and a female, and made you tribes and families that you may know each ; Surely the most honourable of you with Allah is the one among you most careful (of his duty) ; Surely Allah is knowing, Aware." (Quran 49 : 13)

5.37 **Principle of the brotherhood laid down**

The principle of the brotherhood laid down here is on the broadest basis. The address is here to men in general who are told that they were all members of one family, and their division into nations, tribes and families should not lead to estrangement from, but to a better knowledge of, each other. Superiority of one over another in this vast brotherhood does not depend on nationality, wealth, or rank, but on careful observance of duty — Moral greatness and spiritual aggrandisement. Thus the above injunction for the universal fraternity and equality and to consider the entire earth as one human family is of dire necessity to the world so terribly torn apart because of mutual hatred, differences and jealousy and for superiority over each other.

5.38 **Racialism is condemned**

The teachings of Quran warn against racialism and declare the theory of common origin of mankind. This, as a matter of fact, promotes a sense of equality of all races and the human rights to preserve peace and tranquillity on the earth. All the artificial barriers that divide nations, races, mankind, classes, societies, communities should, on all accounts, be eliminated and all should think themselves as one "citizen of the Globe" with a true spirit of love, equality, and justice for all members of the human family. Thus the members of the international community should not have the coveting of the possessions of others, nor the territories of others, nor have lust or greed for powers and dominance. This paves the way for the establishment of a 'New World Order' where peace, tranquillity, equality, fraternity and mutual trust prevails, and domination and subordination is abolished.

5.39 Healthy conjugal relation and safeguard against family breakups

'A' "Men are the managers of the affairs of women because Allah has made the one superior to the other and because men spend of their wealth on women. Virtuous women are, therefore, obedient; they guard their rights carefully in their absence under the Care and Watch of Allah. As for those women whose defiance you have cause to fear, admonish them and keep apart from your beds and beat them. Then, if they submit to you do not look for excuse to punish them; note it well that there is Allah above you, Who is Supreme and Great. And if you fear a breach between spouses appoint one arbiter from the relatives of the husband and one from the relatives of the wife. If the two sides sincerely desire to set things right, Allah will create a way of reconciliation between them, for surely Allah knows everything and is aware of everything." (Quran 4 : 34-35)

'B' "When a woman fears ill-treatment or aversion from her husband, there is no harm if the two make peace between themselves (by means of a compromise); after all peace is the best thing. Human souls are prone to narrow-mindedness, but if you show generosity and fear Allah in your dealings, you may rest assured that Allah will be fully aware of what you do. It is not within your power to be perfectly equitable in your treatment with all your wives, even if you wish to do so; therefore, (in order to satisfy the dictates of Divine Law) do not lean wholly towards one wife so as to leave the other by His vast powers, for his resources are limitless and He is All-Wise and All-Knowing. And everything in the havens and the earth belongs to Him." (Quran 4 : 128-131)

5.40 **Accord and amity in the family**

The above verses containing the divine injunction offer a true guidance to mankind to maintain harmonious relationship between husband and wife and a safeguard against the family break-ups. The Quran has definitely shown the way to preserve and maintain an amity in the family so that there may be less chance of conjugal separation, divorce and family break-ups with an obnoxious problem of rearing and looking after children born in such family. The upkeep of such children becomes a heavy task for the society and for the Government because of the fact that a lack of parental care, and love, proper training and education, such children are destined to lead a life of destitute and poverty and suffer from psychoses and neuroses that consequently induce them to commit crimes and vices and they ultimately become a sore for the society and for the state without doubt a large number of such cases are coming to the fore every day in the modern society.

5.41 **Position of men in the family defined**[11]

The verses of the Quran (4 : 34-35) guide us most scientifically in keeping with the biological truth that men are superior to women in the sense that they have been endowed with certain natural qualities and powers that have not been given to women or have been given in a lesser degree, and not in the sense that they are above them in honour and excellence. Man has been made the manager of the family because of those natural qualities which he possesses, and woman has been made dependent for her own safety and protection because of her natural draw-backs. Such should be the mutual understanding between husband and wife and thus there will be an accord and harmony in the family and consequently there will be healthier and happier growth of the society. No doubt the Quran has given guidance for the easy solution

11. Orme, J.E. In Introduction to Abnormal Psychology, London, Methuen & Co. Ltd., 1971, p. 34.

of the obnoxious problem of family disintegration, of broken houses, of juvenile delinquency and other vices and crimes rampant in the society, which are vexed and knotty problems for the social and medical scientists as well as for the State, responsible to arrest the growth of the family disintegration.

5.42 A tradition of the Holy Prophet[12] about the wife

A tradition of the Holy Prophet is the best commentary on this. He said, "The best wife is one who pleases when you see her ; who obeys your orders and who guards your property and her own honour when you are not at home." Thus it must be asserted that the injunction of the Quran and the saying of the Holy Prophet are most significant for the establishment of a healthy and homogeneous individual home and for the growth of a happy and prosperous society.

5.43 The broadness of the Muslim Faith

'A' "The Messenger has believed in the Guidance which has been sent down to him from his Lord, and those who believe in the Messenger have also sincerely accepted the same. They all believe in Allah, His Angels, His Books and Messengers. And they say, "We do not discriminate against any of His Messengers." We have heard the Message and submitted to it Our Lord, We look up to Thee for forgiveness, Lord, to Thee we shall all return." (Quran 2 : 85)

5.44 No compulsion and coercion in religion

'B' "There is no compulsion and coercion in regard to religion, the right thing has been made distinct from the wrong thing; now whoever rejects taghut[13] (evil) and believes in Allah has taken firm support that never gives

12. Maudoodi, Abul Ala, *op. cit.* p. 325.
13. The Quran uses this word for one who rebels against Allah; see page 179 of the Meaning of the Quran by Syed Abul Ala Maudoodi.

way. And Allah (Whose support he takes) hears everything and knows everything". (Quran 2 : 256-257)

"(O Mohammad), if the Lord has so willed, all men on earth would have joined the faith (but, in His wisdom, He left them free to choose path according to their own understanding). Wouldst thou then compel people to accept the faith ?" (X : 99)

"And do not revile those to whom they pray besides God out of spite. (Remember) we have made each people's ways and doings appear alluring to them. In the end they will all return to their Lord, and we shall then tell them about the truth about their ways and deeds."[14] (vi : 108)

5.45 The creed of Islam is not thrust upon anyone forcibly

The above verses of the Quran are quite clear that the creed of Islam and its way of life is not thrust upon anyone forcibly. As a matter of fact, this cannot be forced upon anyone. It is, therefore, needed that one's attitude towards followers of other religions must be one of broad mindedness, understanding and tolerance. It is a frailty of human nature that every group of religion regards its own ways as the best and cannot tolerate any criticism against it. The only right course for man, therefore, is one of patience and tolerance.

5.46 Show kindness and affection to parents, to neighbours and the needy

"And all of you should serve God and associate none with Him; and show kindness and affection to your parents, and be kind to near relatives, and to orphans and to the needy, and be considerate to your neighbours — kinsmen, and strangers — and to the companions at your side and to the wayfarer and to the slaves in your possession. Believe it that Allah does not like such

14. 68-69, 'The Spirit of Islam', an English translation of Maulana Abul Kalam Azad's Tarjumul Quran by Syed Ashfaque Hassain.

persons as are self-conceited and are niggardly and bid others to be niggardly, and conceal the bounty of Allah that He has bestowed upon them. We have prepared a disgraceful chastisement for such ungrateful wretches." (4 : 36-38)

5.47 Obedience to parents

"And your Lord has commanded that you shall not serve any but Him and to show goodness to your parents. If either or both of them reach old age with you, show them no sign of impatience, nor chide them, and speak to them a generous word. And make yourself submissively gentle to them with compassion and say, "O my Lord, have compassion on them, as they brought me up when I was little". (17 : 23-24)

The Quran lays the greatest emphasis upon the obedience to parents and, beyond doubt, the home is the real nursery in which the moral training of a person begins. The Quran has thus solved the most excruciating problem of old and infirm parents for whom there is no provision of a room in home of the modern society and as such they are deprived of the humane-dealings particularly in these days when there is a cry and call for the protection of "Human Rights".

5.48 Reverence for Authority

"O Believers, obey Allah, and obey the Messenger and those entrusted, with authority from among you. Then if there arises any dispute about anything, refer it to Allah and the Messenger, if you truly believe in Allah and the Last Day. This is the only right way and will be best in regard to the end." (4 : 59)

5.49 Sayings of the Holy Prophet regarding Reverence for Authority

"It is obligatory on a Muslim to listen to and obey the orders of those invested with authority, whether he likes or dislikes it, provided that it is not sinful. However, if he is ordered to do a sinful thing, he should neither listen to the rulers nor obey their orders."[15] (Bukhari, Muslim)

5.50 **Prevention against rebellion and anarchy**

It admits of no doubt that the teaching of Islam requires all men to obey those who are in immediate authority over them and thus nips in the bud all kinds of rebellion, anarchy and indiscipline in the society and for the healthy growth of the democratic outlook of human society.

5.51 **Injunction regarding justice and evidence**

"O Believers, be you the standard-bearers of justice and witnesses for the sake of Allah, even though your justice and evidence might be harmful of yourselves, or to your parents or to your relatives. It does not matter whether the party concerned is rich or poor; Allah is their greater well wisher than you ; therefore do not follow your own desire lest you should deviate from doing justice. If you distort your evidence or refrain from the truth, know it well that Allah is fully aware of what you do". (Quran 4 : 135)

5.52 **Significance of justice and evidence**

No body can deny the importance and significance of justice and evidence. The above Quranic injunction enjoins upon every one to do justice also to bear the standard of justice in order to eradicate injustice and establish justice in its place. As Believers, the Muslims have to gird up their loins to support justice when their support is needed. The justice should be dispensed with, and the Evidence should be without any tinge of partiality or self-interest, or fear or favour in it. The selfless justice and the impartial evidence are the need of the present day society. The Government offices, the political leaders, the social workers, those who are at the helm of affairs, the individual and the

15. P. 337 The Meaning of the Quran, Vol. I by Syed Abul Ala Maudoodi.

groups thus can keep themselves away from social evil of favouritism, nepotism, and injustice so largely rampant in the present day society where the persons of no support and influence have to suffer a lot under the prevailing condition of social injustice.

5.53 All contracts should be written

"O ye who believe ! when ye deal with each other in transaction involving future obligations within a fixed period of time, reduce them to writing. Let a scribe write down faithfully as between the parties; as God has taught him, so let him write. Let him who incur the liability dictate but let him fear his Lord God, and not diminish aught of what he owes. If the party liable to mentally deficient or weak or unable himself to dictate, let his guardian dictate faithfully. And get two witnesses out of your own men, and if there are not two men, then a man and two women, such as ye choose for witnesses, so that if one of them errs, the other may remind her. The witnesses should not refuse when they are called on (for evidence). Disdain not to reduce to writing (your contract) for a future period, whether it be small or big; it is just in the sight of God, more suitable as evidence, and more convenient to prevent doubts amongst yourselves. But if it be a transaction which ye carry out on the spot amongst yourselves there is no blame on you, if ye reduce it not to writing. But take witnesses whenever ye make a commercial contract, and let neither scribe nor witnesses suffer harm. If ye do (such harm), it would be wickedness in you. So fear God for it is God that teaches you. And God is well acquainted with all things. If ye are on a journey and cannot find a scribe, a pledge with possession (may serve the purpose). And if one of you deposits a thing on trust with another, let the trustee faithfully discharge his trust and let him fear his Lord. Conceal not evidence for whoever conceals it, his heart is tainted with sin. And God knoweth all that ye do". (Quran 2 : 282 : 283)

5.54 Courteous greetings

"When a courteous greeting is offered to you meet it with a greeting of greater courtesy or at least of equal courtesy. God takes careful account of all things". (Quran 4 : 86)

5.55 Mutual consultation — Law of Recompense

"Whatever ye are given here is but a convenience of this life but that which is with God is better, and more lasting. It is for those who believe and put their trust in their Lord, those who avoid the greater crimes and shameful deeds and when they are angry, even then they forgive, those who hearken to their Lord, and establish regular prayer, who conduct their affairs by mutual consultation, who spend of what we bestow on them for sustenance and those who, when an oppressive wrong is inflicted on them (are not cowed but) help and defend themselves. The recompense for an injury is an injury equal thereto (in degree) but if a person forgives and makes reconciliation, his reward is due from God; for God loveth not those who do wrong. But indeed if any do help and defend themselves after a wrong (done) to them, against such there is no cause of blame. The blame is only against those who oppress men with wrong doing and insolently transgress beyond bound through the land, defying right and justice. For such there will be a penalty grievous. But indeed if you show patience and forgive that would truly be an exercise of courageous will and resolution in the conduct of affairs". (Quran 42 : 36-43)

5.56 Do not covet the favours which Allah has bestowed on some of you more than others

"And do not covet what Allah has given some of you more than others; the men shall have their due share according to what they have earned and the women shall have their share according to what they have earned. So pray to Allah for this bounty : most surely Allah has perfect knowledge of everything". (Quran 4 : 32)

5.57 Do not devour one another's property

"O Believers do not devour one another's property by unlawful ways (instead of this) do business with mutual consent. And do not kill yourselves; believe it that Allah is ccmpassionate to you". (Quran 4: 29-32)

Thus as it will be evident the Holy Quran provides guidance to mankind in every aspect of his life. The guidance provided is all embracing and covers all walks of human life be it personal, interpersonal or collective, relating to the periods of war or peace and effecting social, political or economic life. The principles laid down for human conduct are not only practicable but are also characterised by justice, balance and fairplay. In fact any deviance from the golden principles is almost certain to lead to disorder, turmoil, conflicts and unhealthy developments in human society. These principles can form the basis of laws to be framed for the successful functioning of a civilised society whether formally Islamic or non-Islamic. It is only through acting faithfully in accordance with Quranic injunctions that a healthy development of a society can take place, banishing conflicts and wars and ushering in an era of peace, prosperity and progress.

APPENDIX I

THE QURAN AT A GLANCE

It contains 30 paras (Parts)
114 Surah and
6666 Aayats (verses) based on 323760 letters

1. The first Revelation was : Surah Alaq
2. The last Revelation was : Surah Albaqra
3. The total period of Revelation was 22 years 5 months and 14 days (based on approximate calculations)
4. Types and number of verses :

Aayate-Wada	1000
Aayat-e-Waeed	1000
Aayet-e-Nahi	1000
Aayat-e-Misaal	1000
Aayat-e-Amr	1000
Aayat-e-Qasas	1000
Aayat-e-Tahleel	250
Aayat-e-Tahreem	250
Aayat-e-Tasbeeh	100
Aayat-e-Motafarraqa	66
Total	6666

5. The places of Revelations were :

Ghare-Hera	(Cave of Hera)
Kohe Safa	(Mountain Safa)
Dare-Arqam	(House of Arqam)
Masjid-e-Jinn	(Mosque of Jinn)
Masjid-e-Qaba	(Mosque of Qaba)

Wadi-e-Badr	(Place of Badr)
Jablul Uhud	(Mountain Uhud)
Moqam-e-Khandaq	(Place of Ditch)
Masjid-e-Qablateen	(Mosque of Qablateen)
Masjid-Sayyadena Amir Hamza	(Mosque of Amir Humza)
Wadi-e-Arafat	(Place of Hajj)
Sha-rul-Haram	(Mashrul Haraam)
Wadi-e-Mana	(Mana)
Majid-e-Fatha	(Mosque of Fatah)
Bait-e-Rizwan	
Masjid-e-Aqsa	(Mosque of Al-Aqsa)
Mada-i-ne-Saleh Altur	(Mountain Tur)
Mountain Zaitun	
Madeen-ka-Kuan	(Well of the city Medina)
The place of the jews court	
The lanes of the Baitul Moqqadus.	

APPENDIX II

COMMENTARIES (TAFSEER) ON THE QURAN

The Quran inspired many scholars to develop a scientific field of study known as 'Tafseer'. It aims at deriving the correct meaning of the Quranic verses, by way of analysing and interpreting the various factors of revelations including need, purpose, objective, authenticity and the circumstances of revelations so that the spirit of the Quranic verses should be understood in the right perspectives. Accordingly, a plethora of literature on this subject has been produced in different languages at different intervals in different parts of the world. The history of this branch of knowledge could be traced as early as the 2nd century Hijrah. The description of some of the important 'Tafseers' is given below :

S. No.	*Name of the Author*	*Title of the book*	*Script*	*Volume*	*Date*
1.	Allama Ibne Jerrerut Tabri	Jame-ul Beyan	Arabic	30	31 Hijrah
2.	Imam Fakhruddin Mohammad ben Umer Razi	Tafseer Mofatihul ghaib	Arabic	8	606 "
3.	Ibnul-jozi	Tafseer-e-Ibnul jozi	Arabic	27	597 "
4.	Abu Zaid Abdur Rahman bin Mohammad Altaabi	Aljauaheral Ahsan fitafseerul Quran	Arabic	—	876 "

5. Allama Jalaluddin Sauti		Arabic	32	911 "
6. Mohammad Abdullah	Ruhul Maani	Arabic	10	1270 "
7. Allama Johari Tantavi	Tafseerul Jawahir	Arabic	25	1359 "
8. Allama Syed Qutb Shaheed	Fizzalalu Quran	Arabic	10	1346 "
9. Ibnul Aqeeb	Tafseer-e-Ibnul Aqeeb	Arabic	50	—
10. Maulana Ashraf Ali Thanvi	Beyannul Quran	Urdu	12	1349 "
11. Maulana Abul Kalam Azad	Tarjumanul Quran	Urdu	12	1349 "
12. Maulana Abdul Majid Daryabadi	Tafseer-e-Majadi	Urdu	2	•
13. Maulana Abul Ala-Maudoodi	Tafheemul Quran	Urdu	4	
14. Maulana Waheeduddin Khan	Tazkirul Quran	Urdu	2	

APPENDIX III

CHRONOLOGICAL EVENTS DURING THE LIFE-TIME OF THE PROPHET MUHAMMAD

571 AD (April 22)		Birth of Prophet at Mecca.
595 AD		The Prophet married to Hazrat Khadija.
610 AD (February 12)	(i)	The first Revelations at Hera 'Recite in the name of the Lord who created! He created Man from a clot of Blood. Recite and the Lord is the Most Bountiful. He who had taught by the pen, taught man what he knew not'.
	(ii)	Khadija embraced Islam as his first disciple.
620 AD	(i)	Married to Hazrat Sauda.
	(ii)	Married to Hazrat Ayisha.
622 AD (September 12)	(i)	Migrated to Medina alongwith his close associate Abu Bakr.
	(ii)	This year marks the beginning of the Islamic Calendar known as Hijrah.

(September 27)	Arrival at Medina.
623 AD	The Prophet promulgated a charter which guarenteed every inhabitant whether migrants (Muhajir) and Helpers (Ansar) including Christians, jews or pagans, equality, civil liberty and religious freedom.
624 AD (March 16)	Battle at Badr which resulted to the victory of the Prophet and his followers who successfully foiled the attack by Meccan tribals.
625 AD (March 21)	(i) Battle at Uhud in which Muhammad and his followers were defeated. (ii) Married to Hazrat Hifsa
626 AD	(i) Married to Hazrat Umma Salma Hind. (ii) Married to Hazrat Zainab daughter of Khuzeema. (iii) Married to Zainab daughter of Hajash.
627 AD	(i) The Meccans besieged Medina in the campaign of al Khandaq. The sudden onset of furious storm and driving sand forced the Meccans to retreat which gave the Prophet much needed respite. (ii) Married to Hazrat Juweeria.
628 AD	(i) Married to Hazrat Umma Habeeba. (ii) Married to Hazrat Safia.

	(iii) The Treaty of Hudaybiah was signed. Accordingly the treaty was to last for ten years.
629 AD	(i) The treaty of Hudaybiah was violated. The Prophet alongwith his ten thousand followers attacked Mecca.
	(ii) Married to Hazrat Maimuna.
630 AD (January 12)	(i) The Prophet got victory at Mecca and occupied the Ka'b'a the house of God.
(February 1)	(ii) The Battle of Hunayn.
(February 3)	(iii) The Siege of Ta'if.
(October/December)	(iv) The Battle of Tabuk.
631 AD (March 9)	Hajjatul Widah i.e. farewell Hajj performed by the Prophet who urged his followers to remain united.
632 AD (May 25)	The Prophet died and was buried in the Masjid-e-Nabawi at Medina.

APPENDIX IV

QURAYSH OF THE HOLLOW

(Fihr is directly descended from Ishmael in the male line. The descendants of Fihr who came to be known as Quraysh of the Outskirts are not shown in the following tree).

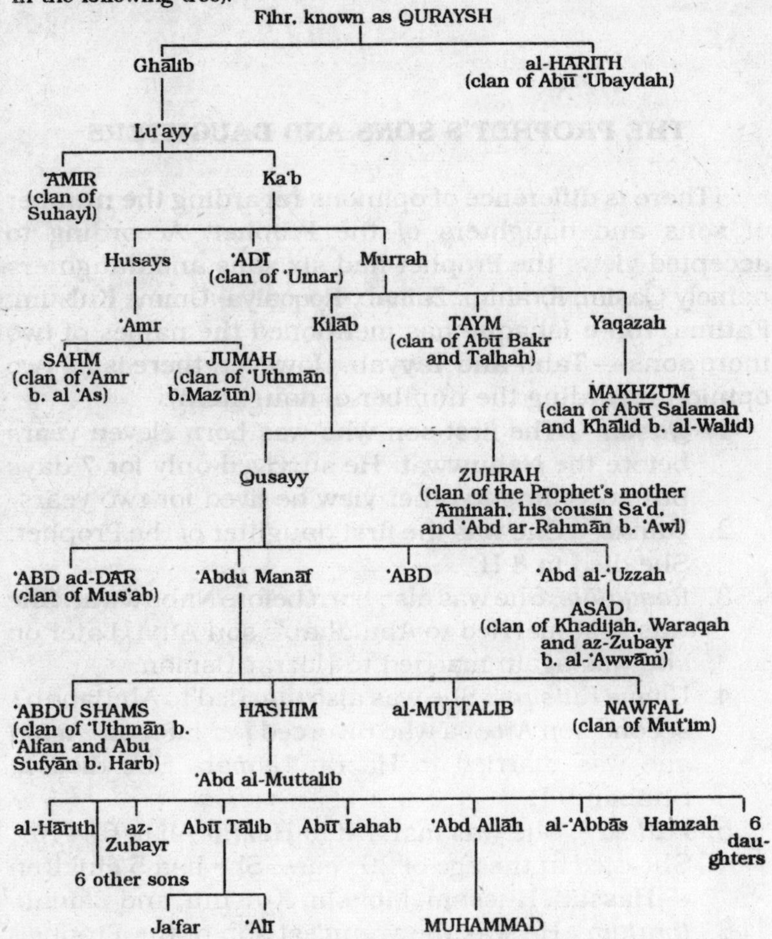

The names of founders of clans are given in small capitals. These are followed by the names of one or more of their descendants who were closely connected with the Prophet or else of historical importance.

APPENDIX V

THE PROPHET'S SONS AND DAUGHTERS

(There is difference of opinions regarding the number of sons and daughters of the Prophet. According to accepted views the Prophet had six sons and daughters namely Qasim, Ibrahim, Zainab, Roqqaiya, Umme Kulsum, Fatima. Ibn-e-Ishaque has mentioned the names of two more sons — Tahir and Tayyab. However, there is no two opinion regarding the number of daughters).

1. *Qasim* : The first son who was born eleven years before the Nabuwwat. He survived only for 7 days but according to other view he lived for two years.
2. *Zainab* : She was the first daughter of the Prophet. She died in 8 H.
3. *Roqqaiya* : She was also born before Nabuwwat. She was first married to Abulahab's son Atba. Later on she was again married to Hazrat Usman.
4. *Umme Kulsum* : She was also married to Abulahab's second son Ateeba who divorced her later on. Again she was married to Hazrat Usman. She died in Shaban 9 H.
5. *Fatima* : She was married to Hazrat Ali in 624 AD. She died at the age of 29 years. She had 5 children — Hassan, Hussain, Mohsin, Kulsum, and Zainab.
6. *Ibrahim* : He was the youngest son of the Prophet. He survived only for two months and ten days. Others believe that he lived for 15 months, or 16 months 8 days or 17 months.

APPENDIX VI

THE ENVIRONS OF MECCA AND MEDIAN

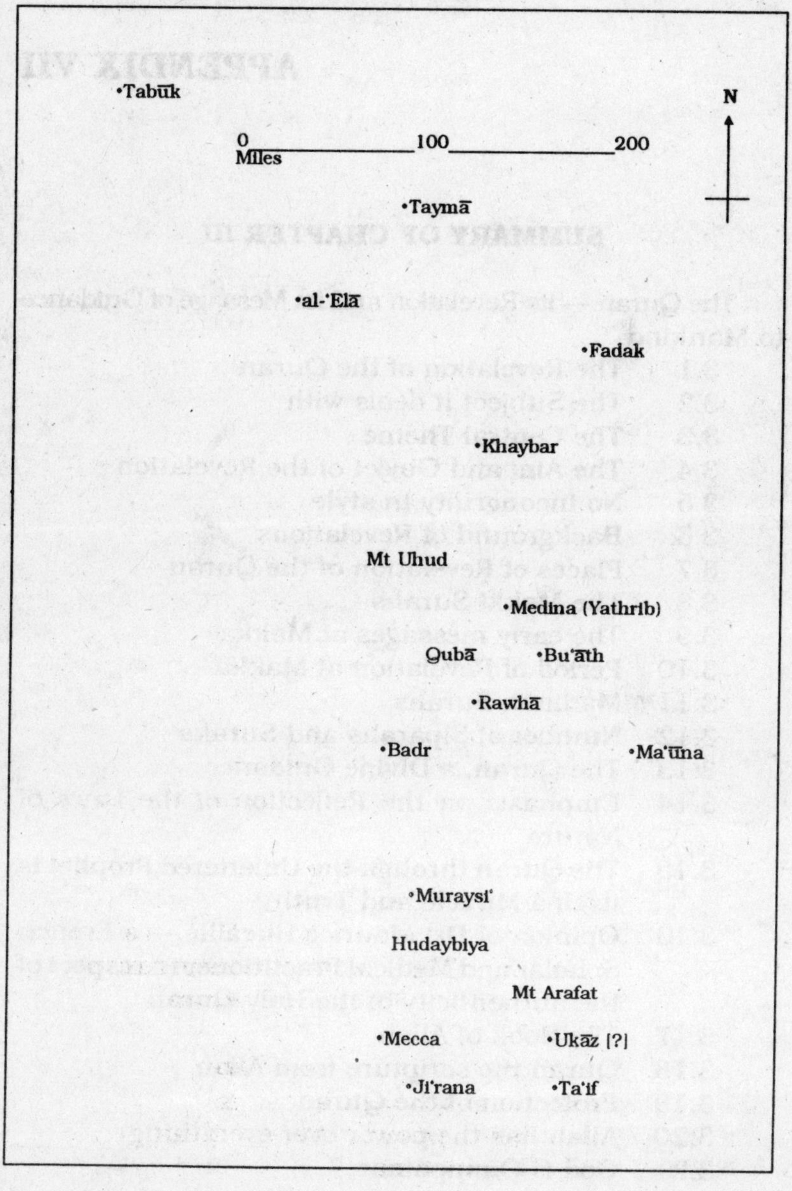

APPENDIX VII

SUMMARY OF CHAPTER III

The Quran — its Revelation and its Message of Guidance to Mankind

3.1 The Revelation of the Quran
3.2 The Subject it deals with
3.3 The Central Theme
3.4 The Aim and Object of the Revelation
3.5 No Incongruity in style
3.6 Background of Revelations
3.7 Places of Revelation of the Quran
3.8 The Makki Surahs
3.9 The early messages at Makka
3.10 Period of Revelation at Makka
3.11 Madinah Surahs
3.12 Number of Siparahs and Surahs
3.13 The Quran, a Divine Guidance
3.14 Emphasis on the Reflection of the Laws of Nature
3.15 The Quran through the Unlettered Prophet is itself a Miracle and Truth
3.16 Opinion of Dr. Maurice Bucaille — a French Scholar and Medical Practitioner in respect of the authenticity of the Holy Quran
3.17 The Book of Allah
3.18 Quran the scripture from Allah
3.19 Protection of the Quran
3.20 Allah has the power over everything
3.21 God is Omnipotent

3.22 God is Omniscient and Omnipresent
3.23 God is Eternal and Absolute
3.24 God knows all
3.25 Trust to God
3.25A Do not walk on the earth with insolence
3.25B Say a right word
3.26 Worthy of honour in the sight of God
3.27 Seek help with Patience, Perseverance and Prayer
3.28 Prayer, Sacrifice, Life and Death are all for God
3.29 The Light of the 'Iman'
3.30 Do not Exceed the limits
3.31 Be Careful of Your Duties and do Good to Others
3.32 Nothing is Hidden from Allah
3.33 Allah Created the heaven and the earth
3.34 Prayer keeps away from indecency and evil
3.35 Every soul must meet death
3.36 Things prohibited
3.37 Worship God and be kind to parents
3.39 God created Man out of mere clot of congealed blood
3.40 All Apostles were but men
3.41 Prophet Muhammad Mercy for all creatures
3.42 The Resurrection
3.43 If there were other Gods besides God
3.44 To God — Sincere Devotion is due
3.45 The Two Kinds of Verses in the Holy Quran

SUMMARY OF CHAPTER IV

Islam — its Meaning, Definition, Origin, History and its Fundamentals

4.1 The Meaning
4.2 The Present Day World and the Necessity of Peace
4.3 Norms of Exchange of Wish Among Muslims

SUMMARY OF CHAPTER V

BIBLIOGRAPHY

Abraham, J.H. (1973)
Origin and growth of Sociology.

Abul Ala Maudoodi, Syed (1982)
Meaning of the Quran Vol. 1 Ed. 3, Delhi, Ruby Printing Press.

Ahmad, Syed Amin (1965)
Spirit and matter reconciled. Islamic Literature Publishing House.

Ahmad, Zahir
Mohammed — Glimpses of the Prophet's Life and Times (Pakistan).

Allen, James (1988)
Prevention of AIDS and H.I.V. infection. Needs and priorities for epidemologic research. American Journal of Public Health V. 78 (4)

Allen, James and Curran, James W. (1988)
Prevention of AIDS and H.I.V. infection. Needs and priorities for epidemologic research. American Journal of Public Health, V. 78 (4).

Ali, A. Yusuf (1934)
Holy Quran, text translation and commentary. Delhi, Kitab Publishing House.

Ali, A. Yusuf (1925)
Making of India. London, A and C Block Ltd.

Ali, Abdullah Yusuf
The Holy Quran, 1968.

Ali, Muhammad
Sahib al Bukhari (Translated into English) 9 Volumes Medina, Saudi Arabia, 1974.

Ali, Syed Ameer (1927)
Short history of the Saracens. London, Macmillan and Co. Ltd.
Ameer Ali
The Spirit of Islam, London, 1922.
Ansari, Fazlur Rahman
The Quranic Foundations and Structure of Muslim Society, Karachi, Feroz Sons, 1975.
Arberry, A.G.
The Quran Interpreted, 2 Volumes. London, 1955.
Azad, Maulana Abul Kalam (1964)
Tarjuma-nul-Quran (Urdu). New Delhi, Sahitya Akademi.
Basheer (1985)
New Delhi, Islamic Republic of Iran Embassy, Vol. 10, 1985.
Brandt, Allen A. (1988)
AIDS historical perspective. Four lessons from the history of sexually inflicted disease. American Journal of Public Health, V. 78 (4).
Bucaille Maurice
Bible, Quran, and science, Urdu translated by Sarjul Haque Siddiqui, Delhi, Taj Company.
Encyclopedia of Americana (1977)
Vol. 15, pp. 491-507. International Edition. New York.
Encyclopaedia Britannica (1973-74)
pp. 911-948. Vol. 9 (Islam).
Freud, Sigmund (1971)
Complete Introductory lectures on Psychonalysis. London, George Allen.
Gauhar, Altaf
Translation from the Quran, Lahore, 1975.
Gibb, Hamilton, A.R. (1962)
Studies on the civilization of Islam edited by Stanford J. Shaw and William R. Polk. London, Routledge & Kegan Paul.
Gilford, Hasting (1925)
Tumours and Cancers; a biological study. London, H.K. Lewis & Co.

Hashmi, Amir Ali
Message of Quran, 3 Vol. New Delhi, Kitab Mahal.
Hayes, Carton J. (1968)
Modern Europe to 1870. New York, Macmillan,
Iqbal, Mohammad (1930)
Reconstruction of Religious Thought in Islam. Lahore, Kapur Art.
Jeelani, Ghulam
Quran (Urdu translation) Lahore, Kitab Mahal.
Jefficoate, Nurman
Principles of Gynaecology, 14th ed. London, Butterworth.
Khan, Maulana Waheeduddin
Ahhyaul Islam (Urdu) Delhi, At Risala.
Khan, Maulana Waheeduddin
Mazheb Aur Science (Urdu) Delhi, At Risala.
Khan, Muhammad Muhsin
A Manual of Hedith, Lahore.
Madhok, Balraj
Indianisation. Delhi, Shiksha Bharti Press.
Mahmud, Y. Zayid
The Quran (English translation) Beirut, 1980.
Maudoodi, Syed Abu Ala
The Meaning of the Quran (translated into English) 4 Volumes, Delhi, 1970.
Mccusker, Jame et al (1988)
Effects of HIV antibaty test knowledge on sexual behaviour in a cohort homosexually active men. American Journal of Public Health, V. 78 (4).
Nadvi, Syed Habibul Haq
The Dynamics of Islam. Durban, Academia, 1965.
Nehru, Jawaharlal (1988)
Discovery of India. New Delhi, Oxford University Press.
New Encyclopedia Britannica
Vol. 7. London, 1973-74.
Orme, J.E. (1971)
Introduction to Abnormal Psychology. London, Methew and Co. Ltd.

Pickthal, M.M.
Meaning of the Holy Quran. New Delhi, Universal Book Stall.

Radiance
New Delhi, 27 Nov.-3 Dec., 1988.

Radical Humanist
V. 51(4) July 1987, New Delhi, Maharani Bagh.

Rapson, E.J. (1955, Reprint)
Cambridge History of India. Vol. I. Delhi, S. Chand & Co.

Rodinson, Maxime (1974)
Islam and capitalism translated by Brian Pearc. London, Allenlane.

Rodinson, Maxime (1971)
Mohammad Tr. by Anne Carter. London, Penguine.

Roy, M.N. (1968)
Beyond Communism. Calcutta, Renaissance Publishers.

Siddiqui, M.K.A. (1984)
Educating a Backward Minority. Calcutta, ABADI Publications.

Sirajaddia, Abu Bakar (1983)
Muhammad, His life based on the earliest sources. Lahore, Evergreen Press.

Sale, George (1934)
Koran. London, Fredrick Warne and Co. Ltd.

Syed Abdul Latif
The Tarjuman al-Quran (edited and translated into English, the Commentary by Abul Kalam Azad (in 3 Vols.).

Smith, Vincent A.
Early history of India. Oxford Clarendon Press.

Smith, Wilfred Cantwell (1957)
Islam in modern history. Princeton, Princeton University Press.

Sayyid, Qutb
Islam — The Misunderstood Religion. Delhi, 1968.

Tara Chand (1954)
Influence of Islam on Indian Culture. Allahabad, Indian Press Publication Ltd.

Watt, Montgomery W.
Companion to the Quran. London, 1967.

Wofferry, E.M. (1979, Reprint)
A comprehensive commentary on the Quran. Vol. 1-3. Ahmedabad.

World Health Organization (1987)
Special programme on AIDS. Report of the meeting on criteria for HIV screening programme. Geneva, 20-21 May, 1987.

World Health Organization (1987)
Special programme on AIDs. Progress Report No. 2. Geneva.

INDEX